Americana:
Folk and Decorative Art

Americana:
Folk and Decorative Art

Introduction by Mary Jean Madigan

Edited by Art & Antiques

An Art & Antiques Book

Produced by Roundtable Press, Inc.

Editorial: Marsha Melnick, Susan E. Meyer
Art Direction: Jerry Demoney
Art Production: Tom Ruis

Catherine Lynn's article, "Bandboxes," is excerpted from *Wallpaper in America*, (c) 1980 The Barra Foundation, Inc., a Barra Foundation/Cooper-Hewitt Museum book, distributed by W. W. Norton, New York, and reprinted here by permission of The Barra Foundation, Inc.

First published in 1982 in the United States by Art & Antiques, a division of Billboard Publications, Inc.
1515 Broadway · New York, New York 10036

Art & Antiques: The American Magazine for Connoisseurs and Collectors is a trademark of Billboard Publications, Inc.

Library of Congress Cataloging in Publication Data
Main entry under title:
Americana, folk and decorative art.
    "An Art & Antiques book."
    Includes index.
    1. Americana. 2. Folk art—United States.
3. Art industries and trade—United States—
History—19th century. I. Art & Antiques.
NK807.A65   745'.0973   81-21606
ISBN 0-8230-8005-6   AACR2

Manufactured in U.S.A.

First Printing, 1982

Contents

Introduction

As anyone who regularly browses through bookstores, attends antiques shows, or keeps up with the trends in interior design will attest, there is a current and widespread enthusiasm for what might be broadly described as Americana—objects of decorative or folk art with a uniquely American flavor. This phenomenon isn't new. It's been building for more than a century. The great Philadelphia Centennial Exhibition of 1876, celebrating the unity of art with industry, encouraged fairgoers to take pride in the American past and in the material culture that documented it. Commercial enterprise was quick to exploit this interest, and by the turn of the 20th century, "Colonial Revival" furniture could be found in many middle-class homes. On a more scholarly level, after 1900 monographs on indigenous American silver, glass, and furniture began to appear. People lucky enough to have family heirlooms took new pride in showing them off.

By 1926, the 150th anniversary of American independence, the first generation of serious collectors—people like Henry Francis Du Pont, Henry Ford, and Francis Garvan—were busily acquiring superlative examples of the American decorative arts. This new area of collecting gained the impress of institutional authority when the American Wing of The Metropolitan Museum of Art, replete with carefully furnished period rooms, opened to the public in 1924. Initially, only those one-of-a-kind, handmade objects exemplifying pre-1830 craft traditions—Philadelphia furniture, Revere silver, and the like—were deemed worthy of attention. But as the decades slipped by and the finest examples of 18th-century artisanship disappeared into museum collections or escalated far beyond reach of the average antiquer's pocketbook, the spectrum of scholarship and acquisitive taste broadened to encompass virtually every sort of artistic, decorative and utilitarian object likely to be found in the American home of a century or more ago. Today, of course, certain categories of collectibles, like Tiffany glass and Stickley furniture, are avidly sought despite the fact that they are not "antique" in the traditional, hundred-year-old sense of that word.

In selecting articles for inclusion in the present volume, the editors of *Art & Antiques* have adopted a deliberately broad definition for the generic term "Americana," giving coverage to those objects and artworks widely used or displayed in the American household through the turn of the 20th century. Our choices have been selective rather than comprehensive, for to adequately represent every category of collectible fitting this definition would require an entire library rather than a single publication. It is important also to point out that many objects of American interest, although widely used in this country, were not necessarily made here. For example, before the mid-19th century, the demand for ceramic tablewares to replace earlier, cruder treen and pewter was satisfied largely by the importation of porcelain and industrial earthenwares. Export porcelain doubled as ballast for virtually every China trade ship laden with tea and silk that departed the port of Canton for American shores, as Susan E. Meyer points out in her article on Canton wares, while across the globe, Staffordshire pottery, transfer-decorated with historic and commemorative scenes to suit the American taste, was shipped over in great quantities from England.

Nor has the selection of materials for this book been confined to handmade, one-of-a-kind objects; to so restrict our definition of Americana would be to ignore the enormous impact of technology on American society after 1820 when new machinery and new sources of power encouraged mass production, bringing a vast array of inexpensive consumer goods within the reach of virtually every American household. Many articles that sell today in the antiques marketplace for surprisingly high sums—certain molded glass flasks, for example—were originally factory-made for just a few pennies' worth of raw materials, and a small expenditure of time.

It is a primary aim of this book to show that a broad range of factors inspired the creation of various types of Americana, and that many means ranging from handwork to factory production were used to shape the objects themselves.

The instinct to imbue even the most banal objects with harmony of color and form, if not outright beauty, is central to human nature—a universal drive that was by no means confined to our American forebears. Above and beyond this innate tendency, however, were certain factors, unique to American society, that dictated the form and decoration of objects made for use and display in the American home. Religion, ethnicity, patriotism, politics, utility, commercial opportunism, and technical progress were a few of these.

Religion, for example, inspired and informed arts as diverse as Edward Hicks's naive paintings, the crafts of Moravian schoolgirls, and the colorful quilts made by women of the Amish sect betwen 1840 and 1935. As John Guttenberg's article explains, Hicks learned technical painterly competence as a carriage maker and sign painter, but it was his deeply held Quaker convictions that lifted his metaphorical series of Peacable Kingdom paintings beyond the realm of the ordinary, to make him one of this country's best-beloved folk artists. In her study of Moravian schoolgirl art, Kathleen Eagen Johnson observes that these charming crafts, ranging from silk embroidery to painting on velvet, were undertaken as a token of thanks to God for his gift of the talent to create beauty; while Ruth Tanenhaus's article suggests that women of the Amish sect may have compensated for the drab and grinding routine dictated by the religious tenets of these "plain people" by making quilts of exceptionally vibrant color.

Ethnic as well as religious factors inspired form and decoration in the American folk arts. Design traditions were often brought over from European homelands: there are, for example, marked differences between coverlets woven in areas settled by the English and by the Germans, according to Madeline Rogers.

Patriotism and politics were reflected in the decoration of many utilitarian objects, including pieces manufactured abroad for export to the American market. As Helen Harris demonstrates in her article on the Staffordshire potteries of the 19th century, many wares destined for the United States were transfer-decorated with patriotic symbols such as eagles and flags and representations of well-known American sites or historic events. Glass flasks were molded with the likenesses of American presidents or other historical figures, according to John Guttenberg; while those most utilitarian of containers—salt-glazed stoneware crocks and jugs—were also embellished with patriotic symbols and slogans, as Ruth Tanenhaus's article reveals.

Sheer utility provided the creative impulse behind some other objects of Americana. Decoys, for example, were fashioned to meet the needs of migratory waterfowl market hunters in the years between the Civil War and 1918, when the mass slaughter of shorebirds was at last outlawed. Bonnie Stretch points out that these whimsical birdforms were regarded primarily as tools by their hunter-carvers, who imbued them with enticing lifelike characteristics to enhance their usefulness. Only recently have decoys been appreciated as folk sculpture; but the finest examples have a marketplace potential of many thousands of dollars.

Commercial opportunity—a utility of sorts—inspired Antonio Jacobsen, a Danish music student who emigrated to the United States, to take up the marine painting for which he is now remembered. Anthony Peluso reveals that Jacobsen was painting nautical decorations on safes to augment his musician's salary when he discovered that the owners of steam and sailing ships would pay handsomely for "portraits" of their craft. Thereafter he became a prolific full-time artist, documenting the vessels that plied the busy port of New York.

Still other decorative objects were created as an antidote to the loneliness and tedium of long, empty days at sea. Scrimshaw, according to Daniel Prince's article, was a favorite pastime of homesick sailors on years-long whaling voyages. Pride in fine craftsmanship played yet another kind of inspirational role in the making of some memorable pieces of Americana like intricately stitched white quilts, which Madeline Rogers tells us were regarded as "the Quilter's final exam."

By no means the least important creative catalyst was technological progress itself—the promise of pleasure or comfort through the application of technical discoveries. The various kinds of oil burning lamps—each one an improvement over its predecessor—that were used in America throughout the 19th century were inspired by the acceleration of technical progress in a rapidly industrializing age, as Joseph T. Butler demonstrates in his comprehensive article. The shape and decoration of these lamps was often dictated by the mechanical requirements of their operation. Similarly, toward century's end, as Joel Levine and Madeline Rogers explain, the invention of the star wheel and flat musical disc encouraged the mass-production of inexpensive disc music boxes that filled America's parlors with glorious resonance and the pleasing glint of engraved, polished brass.

While handwork was important to the development of indigenous American decorative arts, as in the case of scrimshaw or white quilts, it is a fact that most objects—whether decorative or utilitarian—made after 1825 in America bore the impress of the machine to some degree or other. Machine work, in and of itself, is not necessarily bad, as traditional decorative arts scholarship sometimes suggests. Jacquard coverlets, for example, are much prized today for their workmanship as well as the intricacy of their double-woven designs. They were made, however, on large, complex looms fitted with a special set of punched cards that dictated the positioning of the weft threads and hence the pattern of the finished article. With the Jacquard attachment, a weaver could—and often did—complete an entire coverlet in a day's time. Machine-rolled tin provided the basis for colorfully painted boxes and pitchers; pressing machines turned out appealing examples of pattern glass as well as a variety of decorative vessels; while cast iron toys and banks, disc music boxes, and bandboxes covered with brightly patterned wallpaper that was printed on mechanical presses owe their unique qualities to machine work.

Changing patterns of commerce, reflective of basic changes in American society, are evident in the ways by which objects of Americana travelled from producer to consumer. Direct transfer from the craftsman to the customer, by sale or by barter, was only one of the options. In the earliest years of the century—and in rural areas, well into the post-Civil War period—the itinerant peddler played an important role in the distribution of such small craft items as painted tinwares. According to Margaret Mattison Coffin, these colorful containers were made and decorated in home workshops in the mid-Atlantic and New England states, then peddled across the lonely reaches of countryside from farmhouse to farmhouse, in return for a few pennies or whatever goods the farmwife could offer in exchange.

Regardless of the factors that inspired its form and decoration, the means by which it was executed, or the way in which it found a home, every piece of American decorative and folk art tells a fascinating story of times gone by. All across this land, American history endures in textile and tinware, in pottery and glass, and in the painted expressions of a thousand untrained artists. To celebrate the richness and variety of these objects and artifacts—and of the culture that produced them—is the purpose of this book. ■

Edward Hicks

Perhaps the best-known American folk artist, Hicks drew inspiration from his Quaker beliefs. He painted at least 100 versions of "The Peaceable Kingdom" of beasts.

BY JOHN P. GUTTENBERG, JR.

Edward Hicks, painter of *The Peaceable Kingdom*, would have insisted that the Lord's work of his Quaker ministry was the important thing about his life. He would be astonished to learn that his modern audience regards him as perhaps America's foremost early primitive painter.

Today Hicks's work is widely celebrated as the quintessential expression of the 19th-century folk artist. No true retrospective of that genre is complete without the appearance of his infant children surrounded by beasts of the farm and forest, a Pennsylvania farmscape, or one of his many re-creations of patriotic events. We know of almost 160 signed Hicks canvases to date. Yet, despite the approximately 100 he devoted to his favorite subject of "the Peaceable Kingdom of the Branch," Hicks and his life remain relatively obscure. ("The branch" in this Old Testament phrase refers to the branch of Jesse out of which the coming Messiah will emerge.)

The life of Edward Hicks of Bucks County, Pennsylvania, apparently knew little of the serenity that characterizes his peaceful art. His 69 years were liberally traced by spiritual conflict, frail health, and chaotic financial affairs. His paintings at once both mask and explain these conditions.

Hicks was not born into the Society of Friends. Although his family had Quaker roots, his parents and paternal grandfather were Church of England. Their wealth and privilege, accrued from numerous Crown commissions, was swept away in the Revolution. The ensuing deprivation, coupled with his mother's death when he was three, led young Edward into the care of a Quaker, Elizabeth Twining. His formative education consisted largely of her teaching from the Scriptures and though her husband was keeper of the local library (a trunk of books kept beneath the roof of the house), Hicks showed little interest in its content. Many years later he would recall his foster upbringing in his painting *The Residence of David Twining*. In it, he portrays the kindly Elizabeth reading to him beneath a large tree.

Disappointed that his son was ill-equipped to pursue one of the professions, his real father bound Edward as an apprentice to a local carriage-maker at age 13. The shop was in sharp contrast to the sheltered existence of the Twining household. Here Hicks learned not only the rudiments of humble craft, but also the raucous worldliness of the craftsmen who plied it.

When the shop burned two years later, Edward was put to work in the next-door tavern as a "lackey, shoe-black hostler

The Quaker Edward Hicks once described painting as "one of those trifling, insignificant arts which has never been of substantial advantage to mankind." His low opinion did not prevent him from becoming our foremost primitive painter.

Left: *The Residence of David Twining in 1785*, ca 1846. Oil, 26½ x 31½. After his mother died in 1781, Edward Hicks went to live on the Twining family farm, and it was at Mrs. Twining's knee that he was first exposed to the Quaker religion. Hicks can be seen here next to her below the tree in the lower right corner. Abby Aldrich Rockefeller Folk Art Center, Williamsburg, Virginia. Above: *The Cornell Farm*, 1848. Oil, 36¾ x 49. One of Hick's recurring subjects was the landscape of Pennsylvania where he grew up.

The leopard with the harmless kid laid down
And not one savage beast was seen to frown

The wolf did with the lambkin dwell in peace
His grim carnivorous nature there did cease

The lion with the fatling on did move
A little child was leading them in love;

When the great PENN his famous treaty made
With indian chiefs beneath the Elm-tree's shade.

Hicks was a devout Quaker preacher and considered his ministry his most important work. His favorite artistic subject—of which he painted at least 60 versions—was "The Peaceable Kingdom." The subject matter derived from a prophesy in Isaiah: ". . . the wolf shall dwell with the lamb and the leopard shall lie down with the kid." The styles of Hicks's Peaceable Kingdoms went through several stages during his life. Early examples (above and left) reflect the painter's longing for peace. In later examples (opposite page, above) there is a tense and fearful look to some of the animals, perhaps an indication of Hicks's inner torment over a split that was taking place in the Society of Friends. The final period (opposite page, bottom) reveals a mood of tranquility; the animals have a tender, almost weary expression. Above: *A Peaceable Kingdom,* ca 1830. Oil, 32½ x 41½. Philadelphia Museum of Art, bequest of Charles C. Willis. Left: *Peaceable Kingdom,* ca 1842. Oil, 26 x 20½. Private Collection. Opposite page, above: *Peaceable Kingdom,* ca 1842. Oil, 17½ x 23⅝. The Brooklyn Museum, the Dick S. Ramsay Fund. Opposite page, below: *The Peaceable Kingdom and Penn's Treaty,* 1847. Oil, 21⅜ x 28. Yale University Art Gallery, bequest of Robert W. Carle, B.A. 1897. Opposite page, top, right: Portrait of Edward Hicks by Thomas Hicks, 1838. Oil, 27 x 22. Thomas was 16 years old when he painted this portrait of his cousin Edward. Two other versions of the painting exist, all of them were probably presented to family members as gifts. Note the Peaceable Kingdom in progress on the easel. The Abby Aldrich Rockefeller Folk Art Collection, Williamsburg.

and bartender." This even faster company quickly taught him the pleasures of games, frolics, lewdness, and intemperance. By the time the shop reopened, his affinity for spiritous liquors served him well in the customary celebrations that took place upon the completion of a carriage. These festivities called for the consumption of "three or four gallons."

At 18 Hicks found himself enamored of martial music and the featherbed foppery of the regimental dandy. Joining the militia, he quickly took to the off-hours reveling of his drilling comrades. But after a year of being a full-fledged soldier who never saw action, he began to rue his follies and returned to his coachmaker's craft.

Respectability generally bored him, however, and he continued his ramblings with greater frequency and intensity. In his *Memoirs*, he later confessed to a fondness for the company of young women, music, and dancing. Hicks occasionally was lured to nearby Philadelphia for long draughts and debauches. It was on his return from one such trip that he fell seriously ill and narrowly escaped death. Despondent over his errant ways he made his way to the door of the Middletown Friends Meeting House. The spartan environment, plain garments, and silence of its worshipers were fortifying. Clearly it recalled for him the Quaker training of his childhood. He had seen the Light.

Hicks soon entered into junior partnership with a coachmaker in Milford with the proviso that he would have time off to attend midweek meetings. During this period he developed a taste for reading, and the local library records show that he explored Washington's *Letters*, Murray's *America*, Cowper's *Poems*, and Voltaire. In 1803 he joined the Society of Friends and in the same year married his childhood sweetheart.

The lifelong financial hardship he would endure began at once. He borrowed funds to build their home in Milford. The arrival of five children added to his burden. So, too, did his religious calling.

In the Society of Friends one's silent meditation might lead to a conflict between an urge to speak and a trepidation to do so. Edward Hicks ultimately yielded to an inner summons to speak, experiencing great relief in the process. His eloquence earned him praise from his meeting and ultimately led to ministerial travel at his own expense. Journeys to Philadelphia, Baltimore, Wilmington, Virginia, across New York, and even into Canada drained his slender resources.

If Hicks was stirred by Quakerism, then his religious advocacy of humble industry would seem to have been a perfect justification for his craft. Nevertheless, his needs to support his family and his ministry spurred him to discover new sources of income. If his spirit was surviving, his pocketbook was not.

As a coachmaker, he had mastered the art of painting and decorating the vehicles he built. Now he began to put his brushes to more varied tasks. Floor cloths (painted canvas, well varnished), "waggons"—like mobile billboards decorated with advertising—and small pieces of furniture requiring decorative detail were among his first efforts. Soon he began accepting commissions for "directors," or street and shop signs which called for bold, clear letters in low relief. Tavern signs

formed the real bridge between coachmaker and artist, requiring him to draw figures and scenes. Few of these signs still exist, but they clearly taught him to handle modest composition. From these jobs he developed his flair for copying a subject given to him. In time this talent would lead him to imitate the work of others in his own adaptations: *Noah's Ark, Penn's Treaty with the Indians, Falls of Niagara, Washington at the Delaware,* and *The Declaration of Independence.* Similarly, he was known to have painted fireboards (which fit into the aperture of the fireplace when not in use), copied from elaborate landscapes. These, no doubt, were precursors of his pastoral paintings *The Cornell Farm* and *The Leedom Farm.* Most of all, signs and boards were Hicks's first excursions into artistic imagination.

Still, his religious fervor bridled his esthetic impulses. He brooded over his paint jobs because they kept him from the work of the Lord. The quest for "Inner Light" did not bring inner peace. As he worked, his brushstrokes seemed rude interruptions to some inner train of thought—his plight in life, a stirring speech he wished he'd delivered at last meeting, or one he would compose for the next.

He became more dogmatic, intolerant, and righteously indignant of those who disagreed with him. His zeal fired his imagination and his vocal ministry became more inspirational. Hicks was speaking regularly at meetings and funerals away from Newtown, where he now resided. His returns home were unsettling, and he promptly would set out again to preach his itinerant gospel. He despised "gentlemen den-

Throughout his artistic life, Hicks painted patriotic works that celebrated the bounty and promise of a new nation, and landscapes of the countryside near his childhood home in Bucks County, but his religious paintings, based on episodes from the Bible, are the most numerous and enabled him to justify his creative bent among the Society of Friends. Right: *Noah's Ark*, 1846. Oil, 26½ x 30½. Philadelphia Museum of Art, bequest of Lisa Norris Elkins. Below: Study of a Lamb, ca 1831. Pencil, 5½ x 5. Private collection.

tists," "usurers," and doctors—those elevated to the professions through privilege and formal education. They did not fit into his heaven. Among those upon whom he rained down his pieties were the countless creditors from whom he had borrowed heavily to cover his poorly run affairs.

It is believed that Hicks took up easel painting some time after he moved to Newtown. As a self-trained artist he relied on indirect inspiration for all his painting except for most of his farmscapes. Richard Westall, a British artist, was the inspiration for Hicks's famed *Peaceable Kingdom of the Branch*. Westall was a prolific illustrator of New Testament scenes found in the Bible and Common Prayer Book of the day. One of his drawings was entitled *The Peaceable Kingdom* and quotes Isaiah's prophesy of the coming of the Messiah.

Hicks adapted this favorite theme in different ways while preserving its central message. Nearly all versions have localized features—such as Penn signing his famous treaty of peace with the Indians, the Delaware Water Gap, or Virginia's Nat-

ural Bridge—as if to remind his audience that he was speaking directly to them. But each composition was dominated by a scene depicting a trustful child (or children) in the midst of friendly beasts.

"The wolf also shall dwell with the lamb, and the leopard shall lie down with the kid; and the calf and the young lion and the fatling together; and a little child shall lead them." So spoke the 11th chapter of Isaiah. Edward Hicks painted this sermon again and again. His own penchant for verse caused him to translate the prophesy into a verse of his own. He had it printed for presentation to the recipient of the canvas. Occasionally he would print a few lines from the poem on the four sides of the painting's frame.

In the 1820s the Society of Friends was threatened by a deep schism between two factions. The Orthodox emphasized the Bible and the Atonement of Christ. The Hicksites remained adamant in their conviction that faith was secured only from the Holy Spirit, or the "Inner Light," as they called it. The Hicksites were lead by Edward's New York cousin, Elias.

The conflict within the Church gave Edward cause for renewed zeal. His spirited partisanship spawned sincere defense but offended many in the process. A separation in 1827 formally divided the erstwhile peaceable kingdom of the Quakers.

Thereafter, Hicks's paintings took on a new dimension. Increasingly the beasts in his "kingdoms" developed the qualities of human characters. In an 1837 sermon he recalled the belief that all mankind falls into one of four temperaments: melancholy, sanguine, phelgmatic, or choleric. These temperaments, he suggested, are symbolized respectively by the wolf, leopard, bear, and lion. Redemption through the Inner Light, Hicks asserted, would permit each of them to be spiritually transformed into their gentler domestic counterparts—the lamb, kid, cow, and ox.

The simpler appeal here was found in the animal-spiritual, body-soul thesis. Hicks saw the wolf or leopard (animal nature) reposing with the lamb or kid (spiritual nature)—a sure message that humans must strive to recognize the superiority of the spiritual over the animal side in their nature. The stronger philosophical and theological ramifications derived from the notion of the Great Chain of Being which permeated 18th- and 19th-century thought.

Hicks never thought of himself as an artist, much less a scholar. Though he described himself as a "poor illiterate mechanic," his painting assures us that he had the craftsmanship of the artist and the imagination of a creative being. And if his was not a life steeped in learned studies, he did possess a natu-

William Penn was an important, symbolic figure for Hicks, evidenced by the paintings shown here. Above: *Penn's Treaty With the Indians*, ca 1835. Oil, 18 x 24. The Bucks County Historical Society, Doylestown, Pennsylvania. Below: *The Grave of William Penn*, 1847. Oil, 23½ x 29½. Newark Museum, gift of Mr. and Mrs. Bernard M. Douglas, 1956. Right: *The Declaration of Independence*, 1840. Oil, 26¼ x 29¾. Chrysler Museum at Norfolk, Virginia.

ral intellect that enabled him to reflect upon and discuss profound principles and ideas.

As an artist, Hicks was no doubt hopeful that his efforts did not violate the austere restraints of his religion. For Hicks this must have had its compensations. While Friends eschewed beauty in the arts, they appreciated it in nature.

Hicks either gave away or sold most of his paintings to Friends or clients (for whom he painted coaches) in Pennsylvania, New York, and as far away as Virginia. He may have given away some of his paintings as recompense for bed and board while he traveled on behalf of his ministry. Some may have been offerings to pay off debt. Hicks also sold many of his works for what would then have been considered a handsome price for an untrained artist. He received as much as $100 from his cousin Silas Hicks, and $20 from a Friend in

Middletown, Joseph Brey.

Throughout his life he was of a mind that his painting was an unworthy activity for a spiritual man but perhaps necessary to earn one's keep. In his *Memoirs*, he protests that "[my painting] though too trifling and insignificant for a Christian to follow, affords me an honorable and I hope an honest living." Juxtaposed with these deprecatory statements are remarks such as "Diligent at my trade and business, which must be right for me, as it brings me peace of mind."

The seesaw battles he waged between conflict and peace were not those of a mere dreamer-painter. Hicks was, as Professor George P. Winston wrote some years back, "fully a man of his own times, and an excellent example of the Quaker aesthetic in practical operation: a contradiction in that he denied the aesthetic but could not escape the aesthetic impulse, a synthesis of craftsmanship and primitive, professional and amateur—above all, innocent *in* the world, if you will, but never *of* the world."

Edward Hicks, nearly 40 years a preacher and for somewhat longer a humble craftsman-artist, died in 1849. He was reported by a friend to have been happy and peaceful at the end. He was, at last, to enter his beloved Kingdom. ■

Edward Hicks's favorite sermon

The wolf also shall dwell with the lamb, and the leopard shall lie down with the kid; and the calf and the young lion and the fatling together; and a little child shall lead them.

And the cow and the bear shall feed; their young ones shall lie down together; and the lion shall eat straw like the ox.

And the sucking child shall play on the hole of the asp, and the weaned child shall put his hand on the cockatrice's den.

They shall not hurt nor destroy in all my holy mountain; for the earth shall be full of the knowledge of the Lord, as the waters cover the sea.

ISAIAH XI:6–9

A Hicks-modified version of Isaiah

The wolf with the lambkin dwells in peace
 his grim carnivorous thirst for blood will cease;
The beauteous leopard with his restless eye,
 shall by the kid in perfect stillness lie;
The calf, the fatling and young lion wild,
 shall all be led by one sweet little child;
The cow and the bear shall quietly partake
 of the rich food the ear and corn stalk make;
While each their peaceful young with joy survey
 as side by side on the green grass they lay;
While the old lion thwarting nature's law
 shall eat beside the ox the barley straw.
The illustrious Penn this heavenly Kingdom felt
 Then with Columbia's native sons he dealt,
Without an oath of lasting treating made
 In Christian faith beneath the elm tree's shade.

Antonio Jacobsen

A prolific ship portraitist, Jacobsen documented the steam and sailing vessels that frequented the busy port of New York.

BY A.J. PELUSO, JR.

New York was a center of the maritime world in the late 19th century. The city was surrounded by sail and steam ships moving down the Hudson River and up the East River. New York imported and exported more goods, accepted more immigrants, and sustained more steamship and steamboat lines than any other city in the world. Walt Whitman called it the "City of Ships," and Antonio Jacobsen painted them.

Jacobsen was a man of great talent and overwhelming output. Some 2,000 examples of his work, publicly and privately owned, have been catalogued by Mariners Museum in Newport News, Virginia. (This museum also holds the largest collection of his work.) Jacobsen paintings continue to surface, so that it is not inconceivable that his actual output was closer to 5,000. His career spanned more than 40 years, and it is likely that many of his canvases have since been destroyed.

In 1849, when Antonio Jacobsen was born to the Jacobsens of Copenhagen, Denmark, his father planned for him to become a musician. He hoped that his young son would one day use a violin similar to the kind he was known for making. He

wanted the boy to play with his friend Leopold Damrosch, the concertmaster at Wiemer, and to study with his friend and client Ole Bull, a rival of Paganini. As if to ensure the boy's fortune, Ole Bull, who attended the christening, suggested the boy's unique name: Antonio after Stradivarius, Nicolo after Amati, and Gasparo after Bartolotti da Salo—all, like Antonio's father, legendary violin makers.

His father was reasonably prosperous, so Antonio Jacobsen's childhood was uniquely advantaged. Antonio learned to play the violin, viola, and cello, spent time with his uncle, chief steward of the Royal Hunting Lodge at Sorginfire, and attended the Royal Academy of Design. He also helped his father hang unfinished violins to cure in the tower of the Church of St. Nicholas. From this spot, he saw the old canal and the harbor filled with ships from around the world, and spent his allowance on boats which he hired to take him to the ships. All the while, he sketched and painted.

Denmark was then enmeshed in border disputes between the German states and Prussia. With the coming of the Franco-German War of 1870 to 1871, his father's business suffered and Antonio was forced to leave the academy and take a job in a "commercial house." His home was comandeered by soldiers whom his mother had to feed, and the Jacobsens' tenants were forced to move off the property.

Antonio Jacobsen served for short periods of compulsory military training (which he remembered later for fun and pranks) but by 1871 he was obliged to become a full-time soldier for an undetermined length of time. He decided, instead, to flee to America—a move that typified his personal resolve and strength. He had grown to be a man of culture, sensitivity, and talent, and also a man of uncommon will.

His decision broke his heart—he so loved his native land. For the rest of his life Jacobsen recounted its folklore and sang his native songs. He also wept for the lost joys of Danish holidays.

Ole Bull may have helped him decide to come to America. Bull had toured the country in the 1840s and returned in the 1850s to buy land in Pennsylvania. Bull, who was intent on founding a Utopian colony in the United States, may have shared his American adventures with Jacobsen.

When Jacobsen arrived in New York, he had with him a letter of introduction to Leopold Damrosch, who had already settled there. He auditioned and won a spot in the Damrosch orchestra but hardly could support himself on his income. And besides, as he told it, the musicians were mostly German and drank too much beer. He was immediately on the lookout for another job.

Opposite, bottom: *Niagara*, 1877, Oil/canvas, 22″ x 36″. His work of the 1870s is energetic, with rich pigments and careful detail; the boats often seem to be moving uphill. Private collection. Above: *The Albany*, 1883. Oil/canvas, 26¼″ x 50″. In the early 1880s, Jacobsen painted many side-wheel steamers. Albany Institute of History and Art, gift of Wilfred Thomas.

Above: *Aquitania*, 1893, a later and less detailed work. Oil/cardboard. 26″ x 36″. Kennedy Galleries, New York.

Above: *City of Berlin*, 1879. Oil/canvas, 22″ x 36″. Courtesy Smith Gallery, New York. Jacobsen's specialty was the steamer, although he painted all kinds of boats, such as the ship below: *Largo Law*, 1892. Oil/canvas, 22″ x 36″. Courtesy Berry-Hill Galleries, New York.

While sketching one day in Battery Park, he was offered a job with the Marvin Safe Company painting flower garlands on safe doors. A ship broker asked for a safe decorated with a ship as well as the garlands, and Jacobsen was given the assignment. The safe was situated in the storefront window where Jacobsen was watched by passersby as he painted. One day, a well-dressed man stuck his head into the shop and asked Jacobsen to paint a portrait of his ship, then docked in the East River. Jacobsen accepted the commission and delivered the painting in a few days. The man who accepted delivery asked if he was "the fella" who painted the picture. Jacobsen assumed that *fella* was uncomplimentary but held his temper and his tongue and was astounded when the man ordered several more paintings.

By the turn of the century, visualize Jacobsen returning home to Hoboken from New York City—a short ferryboat ride from Barkley Street, Manhattan, and up Hoboken Hill to Palisade Avenue by trolley. He'd have just delivered a handful of paintings to his clients and be ready to enjoy the benefits which hard work and talent brought him: a house full of the latest Renaissance-revival furniture, a collection of rare stringed instruments, and fine leather-bound books. There was also the company of his friends, Fred Cozzens, his sketching companion; James Bard and James Buttersworth, the old masters; the young editor and artist Samuel Ward Stanton; and his most serious rival, Fred Pansing. On Sunday afternoon he invited his musical friends and relaxed for pleasant hours playing chamber music. In addition to all of this, there were his beloved children, Alphonse, Carl, and Helen.

Strangely, the business of painting steamers hardly existed for any artist at the time. James Bard was content to paint Hudson River steamboats, Buttersworth and Cozzens the yachts and important sailing events of New York harbor. These men rarely accepted a steamer portrait commission. The field was Jacobsen's to master until the German Fred Pansing made it a race.

We can see Jacobsen as others saw him in a piece that appeared in the magazine *Marine Journal* on April 2, 1887:

> We recently dropped in on marine artist Jacobsen at his studio on the Palisades overlooking the Hudson, and found this gentleman improving the day, which was a pleasant one, by painting marine pictures at the rate of one every two hours, in the endeavor to catch up with the many orders he had on hand. It is a question if there is another marine artist in the United States or the world that can do as satisfactory work in his line as Jacobsen. He has made himself so valuable as a producer of perfect pictures of steam and sail vessels that those who have been accustomed to patronize him would be "at sea," as it were, should his hand cease to wield the brush. May he be spared to paint the entire new naval fleet, now an established fact, and the new merchant marine fleet in prospective.

His earliest known portrait is of the steamer *City of Mexico* of the Alexandre Line, dated June 1875. Early commissions came from the Old Dominion Line, the Fall River Line, and scores of others which formed the nucleus of his clientele. He even worked for the Czar's Russian Steamboat Company. The firms habitually placed orders for ship portraits as new vessels were added to a fleet. Many paintings served to adver-

Photograph of Antonio Jacobsen. Mariners Museum, Newport News, Virginia.

tise the lines and were hung in hotel lobbies and travel agencies worldwide. Others were done for the captains, owners, builders, and sailors who took them back to home ports. Jacobsen boasted, with justification, that his paintings could be found anywhere "from a mansion to a tavern."

Academic painters marketed their work at National Academy shows, through the Brooklyn Art Association, or through dealers. Jacobsen, however, was not a passive participant in the art marketplace. There were times when he reluctantly allowed a dealer to handle a piece of his work or permitted Wanamaker's to hang a painting of his in the window. But such arrangements were transitory. Actually, he never waited for a commission; he sought them out. His "card" appeared regularly in the *Marine Journal*, advertising his name, address, and occupation—marine artist.

In the early years, he was almost overwhelmed with work. His substantial change in life-style, in so few years, attests to his success. In 1875 he shared studio space with his wife's hairdressing salon at 257 Eighth Avenue in Manhattan. He noted this address on his work, a device James Bard and others had used quite effectively to let people know from whom and from where similar work could be purchased. Five years later Jacobsen owned a fine house on a square block in Hoboken—now Union City—New Jersey. It was close enough to the New York waterfronts for him to deliver his work (which he insisted on doing) and solicit new business. It was also convenient for a captain or seaman to visit him, place an order, and even watch the ship's portrait being painted.

In later years, as interest lagged and times changed, Jacobsen continued to promote his art vigorously. The Seamen's Bank for Savings in New York, long a collector of fine marine art, obtained many of its Jacobsens directly from the artist. In

Steam launches of the 19th century ran on naphtha, and were consequently very volatile. This painting of the steam launch *Adele*, 1886, depicts the passengers and captain in a straightforward, almost primitive manner. Oil/canvas, 18″ x 30″. The New-York Historical Society.

the afternoon, after it had closed, Jacobsen paid visits to the bank. Under his arms he had a number of works, which he placed on the marble counters in front of the tellers' windows for the bank's executives to appraise.

During these years—the early 20th century—Jacobsen strolled West Street in lower Manhattan. The street was bounded on one side by piers and on the other by saloons. In many of these establishments hung his paintings of ships. He kept abreast of shipping schedules and, as the boats docked, he greeted the captain and crew with finished portraits of their vessels in hopes of selling some.

Jacobsen was unquestionably at his best in the 19th century, though some of his 20th-century paintings met the standards of the earlier work. In the 1870s his paintings were most dramatic. He used plenty of pigment and focused on detail. Many of the ships painted in this period run uphill. The waves are energetic and covered with spray, and on steamers generally all the sails are spread. A small body of work in the late '70s and '80s portrays side-wheel steamboats that rank among Jacobsen's best.

In the next decade Jacobsen continued to paint dramatic scenes but he changed the way he painted water. He now achieved a luminous green or blue which successfully suggests translucency, in the manner of the finest academic marine artists. He also experimented during this time, trying three-quarter views, sailing yachts, and moonlight scenes.

The 1890s might be called his tugboat phase. All the tugboats are painted boldly and are colorful and pleasing. He now painted ships parallel to the horizon and no longer running uphill as in the '70s.

In the first decade of the 20th century Jacobsen began to paint formula or perfunctory waves. There are fewer details in his portraits, and after 1906 he frequently used academy board rather than canvas. These works are therefore more vulnerable to deterioration than those on canvas. (Many are, in fact, unrestorable.) Jacobsen painted dozens of sailing ships and clippers then. Yet his 20th-century tugboats are, to some, less pleasing than the earlier ones because they are less dramatic—more mechanical.

In better times, Jacobsen was probably content with a $25 fee for a painting, though it is said he obtained more money occasionally. In the later years, $5 was what he got. In any case, he earned more than the $5 a week Henry Ford paid his workers in those days.

Jacobsen worked fast. While sometimes completing a portrait in hours, he probably averaged two every three days. The businessman in him forced him to find ways to increase production whenever demand required it. He hit upon the expedient of letting his children help. They never painted the vessels, but they did produce many a sky and sea.

Jacobsen painted neither from life nor fancy. If he didn't know the vessel from previous assignments, he first sketched

U.S. Naval Ships at Anchor in New York Harbor, also painted in 1886, has a very different, stately feeling. Three naval ships in the foreground are *Swatara, Tennessee,* and *Van Alia.* A detail is shown on this issue's cover. Oil/canvas, 22″ x 36″. Courtesy the Fine Arts Collection, Seamen's Bank for Savings, New York.

it from life. His son, Alphonse T. Jacobsen, recalled chasing after his father down a wet, sandy beach as he got close enough to sketch a certain square rigger. "Isn't she pretty? Just look at that figurehead nodding to her reflection in the water . . . ," the father remarked to his son. After making his notes, he hurried back to the studio to complete a portrait of the ship because the captain was due to leave on the tide that evening. He recorded all the detail required in sketch books—actually student workbooks with prenumbered pages. He kept some 80 or more books in a long wooden box which can be dated from 1879 to 1918. The storage box came in handy when he received repeat orders. He then rummaged in the sea chest for the appropriate sketch and went to work. Jacobsen had a peculiar method of using a page. Rather than reduce the sketch to the size of the page, he began drawing the stern to a size of his liking and then continued the midships and prow on the next page. Yet he never wasted an inch of space.

For much of his career, he drove himself from commission to commission, often accepting impossible tasks. Once, he filled a rush order for 200 paintings of one ship—the *Olympic.* His frantic pace concerned his family. They doubted he could maintain his health pushing himself that way. Occasionally he vented the pressure with anger, once smashing a painting over his knee rather than allowing it to be lithographed. (He always thought there was more money to be made by shunn-

ing reproduction.) Understandably, when he reached his 60s, he wasn't as able to withstand the pressures, many of which were self-imposed. He suffered from gastritis and became increasingly dependent on alcohol.

Along with Jacobsen's efficiency, energy, and talent, he was blessed with an idyllic home life. When his luck began to change, however, he found life especially difficult to bear. His serious problems began with the sudden death of his wife in 1908, after 40 years together. She collapsed one night at dinner without warning. The kidney disease from which she died had not manifested itself until then. At the same time, the volume of his work began to diminish. Ships were getting bigger, but there were fewer of them, and tall ships were almost an anachronism. (The sea had become less important to commerce.) These changes made it difficult for him to maintain his accustomed life-style. On top of everything, in 1917 a fire nearly destroyed his home. In May of the next year, World War I took away his two sons, an ironic twist for a man who had left his own father to avoid service in another war. The boys returned safely, but Jacobsen felt alone. He died of a stroke on February 2, 1921.

Borrowing a phrase from Samuel Taylor Coleridge, Jacobsen wrote in his sketchbook that "no more than a painted ship on a painted ocean remains of a great merchant marine." It would have given him great comfort to know that most of those painted ships were his. ■

Decoys

Authentic shorebird decoys were made before 1918—when hunting these wildfowl was outlawed. This singularly American folk art was born out of the country's natural abundance.

BY BONNIE BARRETT STRETCH

When a decoy sold at Sotheby Parke Bernet in 1978 for $12,500, many people knowledgeable about other American art and folk art shook their heads and wondered why. But decoy lovers had no trouble understanding this extraordinary price. The bird in question was a Canada goose that exemplified the attributes of the finest decoys. On the water or on the mantel, the grace of its form and the serenity of its mood are unsurpassed. A strange vitality reverberates in the tilt of the body and the angle of the neck and head. Its warm, tactile surface retains enough of the original paint to create a luxurious, weathered patina. Paint and wood grain, polished by the elements of wind, water, and time, blend together in a natural aging process from which the decoy and the bird itself seem to emerge as a single spirit.

Decoys of this quality, of course, are rare. Of the millions of tollers or stools (as they are also called) that were carved in the heyday of wildfowl hunting in the last century, the vast majority were simply dull blocks, awkward and expressionless. But there were many carvers, some known by name and others anonymous, who sought instinctively or deliberately to distill and heighten in their work the essential character and spirit of the wild creatures they knew so well.

Adele Earnest, collector, critic and author, has written: "The great decoy is a rarity but it can still be found. It is more than an efficient tool, more than a replica of a bird. It is a unique, creative statement made by one man out of his need, with his observation of the natural world and his skill in expressing that vision. . . .

"The wooden decoy appeals to us today, not simply because it was a hunting device, but because in the making, in the carving and the painting, the hunters satisfied their natural need for expression, their need to create. And so, a folk art was born."

It is a folk art that is singularly American, born out of the unique natural abundance of this continent and shaped by both the pastoral romance and the brutal commercialism of our 19th-century history. Up and down the continent every spring and fall there once flew the largest migrations of wildfowl the world has ever known. It is said that a flight of geese or ducks could take all day to pass and then darken the moon by night. American Indians were the first to devise decoys, using mud and rushes and vegetable paints, to entice these succulent high-flying birds within range of bow and arrow and into the cooking pot. The European newcomers picked up the idea early on. (In Europe, where game was scarce and hunting was restricted to the nobility, wildfowl hunting took very different forms.) But it was the advent of the market-gunning system in the middle of the last century that propelled decoy making into prominence as a craft that was often elevated by individual carvers to the realm of art.

The commercial market gunner supplied fowl for the tables of the rapidly expanding American population, and with rapid-fire guns in use after the Civil War, one man could often kill over 200 birds in a single day. This slaughter, based in part on the assumption of an inexhaustible supply of game,

On this page: Sandhill crane, attributed to Charles E. "Shang" Wheeler, ca 1928. A crane was often used as a "confidence decoy" to lure geese, since cranes frequently act as lookouts while wild geese feed. Wheeler's decoys, with their simplicity of form, perfectly proportioned bodies, and delicately shaped heads, have long been prized by sportsmen and art collectors. This example is crafted of polychromed white pine. It was probably made in Stratford, Connecticut, the home of some of the most famous decoy makers of the early 20th century. Abby Aldrich Rockefeller Folk Art Center.

On this page: Old squaw drake, Lothrop Holmes, ca 1890. Decoy carvers clearly worked not only from need but also from love. They experimented endlessly with types of wood and methods of carving, and with relationships between contour and volume. Here Holmes, of Kingston, Massachusetts, used canvas stretched over a wood frame. Museum of American Folk Art, New York. Gift of Alastair B. Martin.

went on for half a century. It was finally halted in 1918 by the Migratory Bird Treaty Act, which capped previous protective laws by an agreement with Canada prohibiting the indiscriminate shooting of birds over their entire range of migratory flight. The greatest wildfowl hunt in history had come to an end.

Nonetheless, with true American paradox, it was market gunning that fathered the art of the decoy. Hunters and guides, baymen and rivermen produced a variety and quantity of decoys exceeded only by the birds themselves. Sea ducks were the most numerous, but there were also thousands of marsh ducks, brant, geese and shorebirds, and even some gulls, herons, egrets, swans, owls and crows, each adapted in style and construction for every kind of local hunting condition along the Atlantic Coast from Nova Scotia to Virginia and in a number of regions in the Midwest.

The first aim of the craft was to make a simple piece of practical equipment, something that could be repeatedly tossed into a boat, set out on the sea, or stuck up on a stick in a marsh. But the successful luring of birds was not a simple matter, and in the market-hunting days when competition was keen, the professional hunter soon learned the difference between a poor decoy and a fine one. When the bay was full of gunners and batteries of stools stretched end to end for miles along the coast, the hunters quickly saw whose decoys called the birds and whose did not.

Clunkers abounded, but each region had its own few mas-

ter craftsmen. For the collector, the litany is long and complex, involving not only the names of carvers but the names of birds and places, often backwater towns otherwise totally obscure. For example, there is Harry V. Shourdes (1861–1920) of Tuckerton, New Jersey, who was probably the most prolific carver of all times and whose greater scaup, black ducks, brant, and Canada geese set the standard for the region. His neatly carved lightweight forms, once piled by the dozens into "sneak boats" to be carried out and set in long shooting batteries along the Jersey coast, are collectors' prizes today.

One of the most revered carvers is Elmer Crowell (1852–1951) of East Harwich, Massachusetts. The natural poses and subtle painting techniques, especially of his shorebirds—including plover, yellowlegs, curlews, sanderlings, and dowitchers—are unexcelled. His early, most fully modeled works are special prizes for which collectors happily sacrifice greatly when they can find them. When the Migratory Bird Treaty Act ended the need for working shorebird decoys in 1918, Crowell turned his hand to decorative carving, which for collectors is wholly different from the art of decoy making.

From Maine to Virginia the lists of names continue. In Accord, Massachusetts, Joseph W. Lincoln was famous for his Canada geese, scoters, and old squaws. On Martha's Vineyard, there were H. Reyes Chadwick, Ben D. Smith, M. H. Mayhew, and Jim Look, among a dozen others.

Along the quiet salt marshes and tidal ponds of Long Is-

This page: Sleeper, Mitchell La France, 1877. A duck in a resting position, from Louisiana. Abby Aldrich Rockefeller Folk Art Center.

land's Great South Bay, shorebirds, or "snipes," were stalked in shallow punts and lured by a variety of serenely posed "stickups"—decoys supported on a removable leg-like stick seated in the body and thrust into the ground. The attitudes and habits of these delicate and varied species are immortalized in the work of numerous carvers such as Obediah Verity, Bill Bowman, John Dilly, and Thomas Gelston, each commanding his own inlet, each observing the same birds and capturing their essence with his own vision and skill. As one observer put it, "The product varied with the individual like handwriting."

Among the men who worked the Delaware River region were John Blair, John Dawson, and Charles Black. In Virginia, Nathan Cobb gave each of his carvings an individual character and pose, and chose his wood so well that the decoys remain in near perfect condition after more than 70 years. In Maryland, a famous pair of brothers, Lem and Steve Ward, carved handsome working duck decoys until the mid-1960s. And in Henry, Illinois, Charles Perdew turned out a variety of decoys representing nearly all the wildfowl in his region, including crows, robins, and cardinals, in addition to such staples as mallard and pintails.

These are the classic names, the carvers whose work became widely known and appreciated during their lifetimes around the turn of the century and whose fame endures today, when names are an important aspect of art collecting. There were, however, many other craftsmen who worked in

more private times and whose names have often been lost to history, but whose quality of workmanship and imagination equals that of the better-known carvers. On Nantucket, for example, there were numerous carvers, still anonymous, who worked early in the 19th century when both time and birds were more plentiful. Shorebirds of all species landed here on the continent's easternmost island, and decoy carvers caught them all in works that display an almost infinite variety of poses and styles. In a collection of several dozen of these lively creations, no two are exactly alike. By the end of the century, many of these birds were exceedingly rare, and the lovely Eskimo curlew was gone from the pantheon forever. Today several decoy enthusiasts are devoting much time to tracking the identities of these highly individual craftsmen and their works.

It is part of the excitement of the field that the list of decoy carvers and their birds is long and incomplete. But the point remains the same. These were men who clearly worked not only from need but also from love, who experimented endlessly with types of wood and methods of carving, with relationships of contour and volume, with color tones and patterns, to create not a replica but the illusion of a living bird.

This illusion of life caught in sleek, symbolic forms is what charms today's folk art collectors and calls up comparisons with African, Asian, or primitive art. But it is important to remember that the elegance and charm of decoys are the products of practical demands of a hard and complex trade. It

was not esthetics or a mysterious primitivism that inspired the abstract shapes admired today, but the need for a sturdy toller that could stand up to hard wear. Realistically carved details were not needed to catch the eye of a flying bird and moreover were subject to breakage; smooth, simple lines were more durable. Complex plumage patterns, also unnecessary, were tricky to repaint season after season; a few key strokes of the right colors in the right places sufficed.

Details that did count were the set of the head on the body, the shape of the bill, the angle of the neck, the way the bird rode the choppy seawater or nestled in the inland bays. On the unsheltered waters off the coast of Maine, hunters used large, heavy sea duck tollers cut from solid wood, with flat bottoms and full wide breasts to provide extra bouyancy and visibility among the rough gray waves. Eider, coot, old squaw, and merganser were favorite species. On the Housatonic River at Stratford, Connecticut, around the middle of the past century, Albert Laing (1811–1886) revolutionized decoy making when he developed a sleek, hollow, low-lying bird with a high-riding breast that pushed the decoy over, not under, the slush and ice of the early-winter Long Island Sound. The elegance and practicality of his form was carried on into this century by two other master carvers—Benjamin Holmes (1843–1912) and Charles "Shang" Wheeler (1872–1949). Wheeler's black ducks, with their utter simplicity of form, perfectly proportioned bodies, and delicately shaped heads often curved into sleeping positions, have long been prized by sportsmen and art collectors alike.

Nonetheless, until recently few folk art authorities have considered decoys as a mature and diversified art form worthy of serious study. Yet these carvings would seem to fall easily within accepted definitions of the field. Folk art has been characterized variously and vaguely over the years, but certain attributes seem agreed on: It is the work of untutored artists who created first out of need, for a utilitarian purpose, and secondly out of love. Thus, in addition to its esthetic value, folk art often reflects and records important aspects of American social history. As Holger Cahill wrote in his introduction to the 1932 catalogue of the Abby Aldrich Rockefeller Folk Art Collection, "Folk artists . . . tried to set down not so much what they saw as what they knew and what they felt. Their art mirrors the sense and sentiment of a community, and is an authentic expression of American experience." This description readily embraces the art of the decoy makers.

It was not until the mid-1960s, however, that the decoy received major treatment in this context. Adele Earnest was the first to write in depth of decoys as an art form, and her 1965 book *The Art of the Decoy* is mandatory (and delightful) reading for even the most casually interested collector. In 1969 The Metropolitan Museum of Art in New York displayed a pair of sophisticated merganser ducks carved by Capt. L. T. Holmes of Kingston, Massachusetts (1824–1899), the museum's first acknowledgment of decoys as art. Recently, several major art institutions—including the Museum of Ameri-

This page: Canvasback, maker unidentified, ca 1910. This decoy, of carved and painted wood with a glass eye, probably originated in Wisconsin. The markings on the bird are clearly those of a canvasback, but the long neck and high head give it an overall profile more characteristic of a goose. Abby Aldrich Rockefeller Folk Art Center.

can Folk Art in New York, the Abby Aldrich Rockefeller Collection in Williamsburg, Virginia, and The Museums at Stony Brook on Long Island—have recatalogued and expanded their decoy collections based on new interest and new information generated in the past few years.

For the most part, however, appreciation from the institutions and authorities of art and folk art has been slow in coming. The prodding of a few knowledgeable dealers and collectors, together with the new respect gained by rising auction prices, has placed decoys on firmer ground as art objects. But the real experts in this field still tend to come not from the world of art but from the world of the hunt.

The major authorities whose writings have national scope are Joel Barber (*Wild Fowl Decoys*, 1932), William J. Mackey (*American Bird Decoys*, 1965), and George Ross Starr (*Decoys of the Atlantic Flyway*, 1974)—all gentlemen sportsmen who found in decoys a romantic link to a bygone era they recalled from childhood, when men waited in boats at dawn for the birds to come over and taught their sons how to call them in to shooting range. Their books, together with that of Adele Earnest, are the gospels of decoy collecting.

But decoy collecting remains a relatively friendly, intimate field, and local authorities can still be found in many sea towns and villages along the Atlantic coast. These are baymen, fishermen, hunters, and carvers who know the water, the weather, the seasons, and the birds, who know how and why the local "coys" were made and often knew some of the

old-timers who made them. They regularly turn up new information about carvers and their work and publish it in such journals as *Decoy World, North American Decoys*, and *The Decoy Collector's Guide*, or in handsome, privately published books. Such avid research keeps the field ever changing, demanding, and fascinating for the alert collector.

Finding these men and talking and trading decoys with them, roaming tidewater villages, and poking around ramshackle boatyards is part of the mystique of collecting decoys. In Joel Barber's day, many a prize could be found this way, old masterpieces abandoned in gunnysacks, heaped in the back of salty boathouses and forgotten after some long-ago last hunt. But the days of this kind of discovery are gone. As William J. Mackey observed, the wildfowl had been overfished and overgunned and now the decoys have been overcollected. Most of the best birds long ago disappeared into many private collections.

Nonetheless, patience and passionate interest have their rewards. Among them is a gradually acquired intuitive sense for decoys that no formal study can provide, another is gradual admission to the decoy fraternity, a rather tight circle of men, and a few women, of all backgrounds who devote most of their free time to buying, selling, and talking decoys.

Many of these people can be found at the big "meets" that occur each year, such as the Midwest Decoy Collectors Association meeting in Chicago and the Easton, Maryland, Wildfowl Festival—massive gatherings of carvers and collectors

This page: Top, Canada goose, maker unidentified, ca 1920. "The great decoy is a rarity but it can still be found," writes Adele Earnest. This bird, one of the finest examples of the craft, sold for a record price of $12,500. Courtesy Sotheby Parke Bernet, Inc., 1978. Middle, merganser female; bottom, merganser male. Maker unidentified, date unknown. Both decoys were crafted from leather and painted wood. Abby Aldrich Rockefeller Folk Art Center.

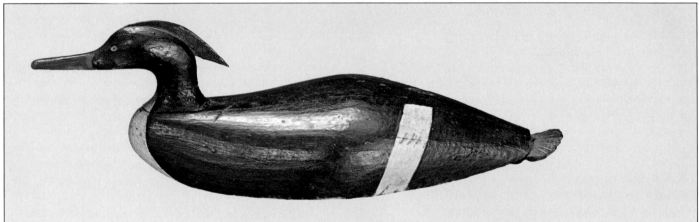

who show their wares, pick up on the latest research and gossip, buy and swap decoys, guns, and hunting memorabilia, and generally talk hunting, carving, and decoys. These are important events for decoy buffs, unparalleled opportunities for acquiring and learning.

They are not, however, the favored environment of most folk art collectors, who are seldom avid outdoorsmen fond of the blood sports of hunting and fishing. Nonetheless, to acquire the knowledge needed for full appreciation of the art of the decoy, one must learn to bridge both worlds, and there are many ways to meet the full range of knowledgeable collectors and dealers. One means is through the *National Directory of Decoy Collectors*, a biannual publication featuring a comprehensive list of decoy enthusiasts and authorities with names, addresses and telephone numbers.

One young collector, Jeff Waingrow of New York City, called up Adele Earnest one day several years ago and took his handful of newly acquired decoys out for her to look at. She greeted him warmly, said his decoys were awful and told him why. He got rid of them and started over. He followed up the names of other dealers and collectors in the region and went around to talk with them.

One of these was Charles "Bud" Ward, of Oceanside, Long Island, a long-time bayman who knows by the feel of the decoy in the hand, the choice of wood for the bill, the kind of nails used, and the paint whether the bird is "right."

The question of rightness or authenticity is an important one, for there are many people dealing and collecting who do not always know what they are selling or buying; in addition, there are occasional outright fakes. The ability to know if a bird is right is a talent everyone agrees is acquired only by experience. It is an educated sixth sense gained by seeking and handling thousands of decoys over many years.

Part of the process of learning for every serious decoyist is a pilgrimage to the Shelburne Museum in Vermont, where the collection of the late Joel Barber now resides. But while increasing numbers of decoys are on view in public museums, a far greater number of prizes are still held in private collections, and it is necessary to see as many of these as possible.

There are collections of all sorts—many focusing on an individual carver, a particular region, types of birds, unusual constructions; others are totally eclectic. There is no one way to collect. A great collection, whatever its focus, is made up quite simply of great decoys.

The fully comprehensive collection, including carvings of all the categories of birds and representing most of the important carvers and outstanding regional work, is unusual. Probably the greatest one of all time was that of William J. Mackey. This vast collection of about 3,000 birds was auctioned off over a period of two seasons at Richard Bourne's in

Hyannis. Mackey was an omnivorous collector who acquired every kind of decoy from a $10 clunker to a $10,000 prize.

The summers of the Mackey sale, 1973 and 1974, were the turning point for decoys in the art world. The collection was famous among sportsmen and folk-art enthusiasts alike. For the first time the prices of decoys were bid up regularly into the thousands of dollars. Everyone was there, and while the auction proceeded inside, an informal swap meet developed in the Bourne parking lot, which has now become an annual summer tradition.

In 1978 Bourne's offered another collection of importance, comparable to Mackey's but of very different character. The collection of Stewart Gregory embraced a broad range of great folk art and included an unusually large number of excellent decoys. Most of these were sold at Bourne's summer auction for record prices, but a few were held by the Gregory family until the following January and were sold at Sotheby Parke Bernet. Among these was the $12,500 goose, whose place of origin is uncertain, whose carver is unknown, but whose beauty is easily recognized by all.

It is still a long way between the worlds of Easton, Maryland, and Sotheby Parke Bernet, and what attracts a true decoy buff does not always appeal to the folk-art collector. Within the limitations imposed by the trade, the decoy artists developed an astonishing range of styles, constructions, painting techniques, and esthetic feeling that makes decoy collecting a very complex and specialized matter. To fully comprehend the field demands a broad sensibility. It requires the roaming of back bays and boathouses as well as Madison Avenue galleries and wealthy homes and penthouses.

Those who would enter this world must enter it wholly. They must first see the beauty of the object, but they must then learn of wood and carving techniques, the habits of birds and the habits of hunters, and fall in love with the romance of 19th-century seacoast history. For the sophisticated collector, a true decoy is not merely a lovely wooden carving but a door through time that reveals the whole life of an earlier period and trade.

Here the most knowledgeable enthusiasts from both the art and the sports worlds meet. The language they choose to speak is different—Adele Earnest may talk of form and line and tonal values of weathered paint; Bud Ward may talk of tools and wood, the behavior of birds, and how a decoy should look on the water. Yet each hears and understands what the other is saying. And in both, one senses a depth of passion for these remarkably beautiful and varied sculptures that have immortalized both our diminishing wildfowl species and the way of life that formed around them. It is an art form that could have happened only in America, derived from a simultaneous love and exploitation of untamed nature. ∎

Scrimshaw

Long, empty hours at sea were turned to good use in these delicately carved souvenir objects of whale's teeth and bone.

BY DANIEL PRINCE

To wile away lonely hours on their long sea voyages, New England whalers carved and decorated countless whimsical objects of whale ivory and baleen for their loved ones back home. The products of this once-humble occupation, now caught in a morass of legalistic interpretation, have enjoyed ever-growing popularity among collectors, nautical buffs, and scholars in the last decade or two. President John F. Kennedy fueled this interest by displaying his personal collection of 36 decoratively incised whale teeth in the Oval Office. During the late 1960s and early 1970s scrimshaw connoisseurship took a back seat to commercial speculation, as prices escalated rapidly. The demand for antique pieces grew more urgent after the passage of the 1973 Endangered Species Act, which restricted the interstate sale of whalebone and whale ivory—or teeth. It became increasingly difficult, and in some cases illegal, to buy scrimshaw objects after that year.

Origins: the name of the craft

The term *scrimshaw*, like so much else about the craft, has been a disputed matter. It is first mentioned in the log of the whaler *By Chance* in 1826: "All these 25 hours of small breezes and thick foggy weather, made no sale [sic]. So ends this day, all hands employed scrimshonting." At least ten other phonetic variations of the word appear in various logs. Herman Melville speaks of the "skrimshander" in *Moby Dick* (1851). Another writer, Clifford Ashley, hypothesizes in *Yankee Whaler* that *scrim* is a colloquial version of *scrimp*—to economize by using up all the scrap parts of the whale—while *shaw* or *shand* refer to sawing or sanding. One group of theorists believes the term is derived from British slang for loafer—*scrimshank*.

Although many of the world's ancient peoples valued whale ivory, which they collected from beached carcasses or found washed ashore with storm tides, the arctic Eskimo were probably the first to carve pictures and decorations on similar materials, such as walrus ivory and bone. However, their work probably did not have a direct influence on the Yankee whalers, who were carving scrimshaw objects long before their ships sailed around Cape Horn and into the Bering Straits, bringing contact with the Eskimo. It has been theorized, but remains unproven, that American seamen learned the art of whale-ivory carving from the artisans of Dieppe, when they were imprisoned together by the British during the Napoleonic and the Revolutionary Wars. The earliest documented piece of American work is signed "Nath'l Healy, 1776." There are fifteen other known pieces bearing inscriptions dated before 1825.

Alone among the many varieties of whales, the sperm whale ranges far out to sea and possesses a 20-foot-long jaw enclosing as many as 50 teeth. (Other whales have long slats of baleen, but no teeth, that they use to sieve their food from the ocean waters.) Sperm whales, bearing the rich spermaceti

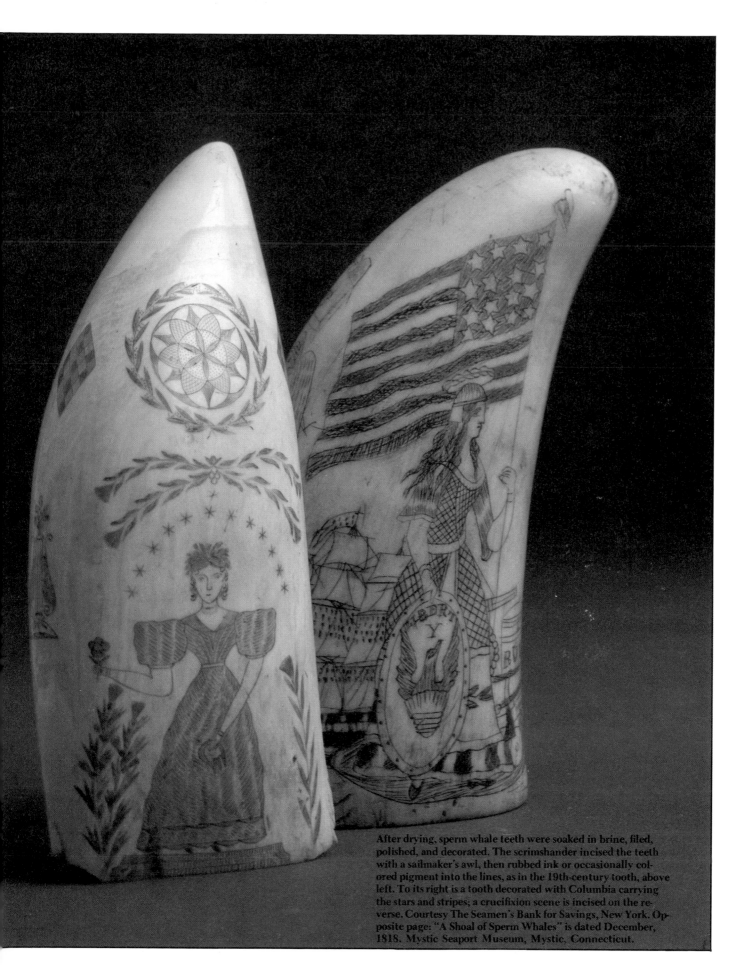

After drying, sperm whale teeth were soaked in brine, filed, polished, and decorated. The scrimshander incised the teeth with a sailmaker's awl, then rubbed ink or occasionally colored pigment into the lines, as in the 19th-century tooth, above left. To its right is a tooth decorated with Columbia carrying the stars and stripes; a crucifixion scene is incised on the reverse. Courtesy The Seamen's Bank for Savings, New York. Opposite page: "A Shoal of Sperm Whales" is dated December, 1818. Mystic Seaport Museum, Mystic, Connecticut.

The Susan on the Coast of Japan

Death to the living   long life to the killers
Success to sailors wives & greasy luck to...

oil used for lamp fuel, were the Yankee whaler's specific prey. These aggressive, unpredictable creatures were highly dangerous: few ships returned from years-long whaling voyages without a fatality. Many ships were rammed and sunk by sperm whales, supporting the whaler's credo: "A dead whale or a stove boat." Nevertheless, the big mammals were intrepidly hunted for their rich cargo of oil; and after their carcasses had been cut up and the blubber tried in large pots on deck, the remaining scraps of baleen and the rare, prized teeth were distributed to the seamen to carve as they pleased. Ridged and stained, the sperm whale's teeth radiate power. They are large, weighing as much as four or five pounds apiece. Even when the ridges are sawed away and carefully sanded with pumice and sharkskin, the creamy ivory retains its shape and glows with an inner life.

The feminine inspiration

On the long voyage homeward, the whale's teeth—or "ivory"—and pieces of whalebone, or baleen, were worked at odd hours, when there was nothing else to do. Most objects of scrimshaw were created for the folks ashore. Teeth decorated with likenesses of absent wives and lovers represented dedication to the ladies. Incised with sailmaker's needles, the women on these teeth are wide-eyed with innocence and the surprise of seeing their men returned from the sea. These clean, tidy female figures don't overwhelm the teeth they

Carving souvenirs from the teeth of the massive mammals they hunted was a favorite pastime of early American whalemen, who almost never thought to sign or date their scrimshaw. An exception was Frederick Myrick, who inscribed his name on many of the pieces he carved aboard the whaler, Susan. Above, top: Myrick's depiction of "The Susan on the Coast of Japan," signed and dated January 2, 1829. Homesick sailors longed for the pleasures of shore life: on the mounted pair of teeth, above, ca 1890, a man and a woman greet one another. Both Peabody Museum, Salem, Massachusetts.

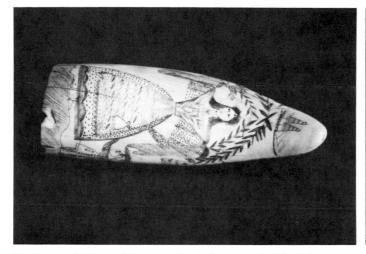

The figures of Adam and Eve decorate the bottom end of the baleen busk—or corset stay—at the top of the page. Kendall Whaling Museum, Sharon, Massachusetts. Whalebone or baleen, a horny substance found growing in the mouths of whales, was used for flexible items such as whips or busks.

Above, left: The figure of a woman holding a child's hand is etched into this whale's tooth. Courtesy Sotheby Parke Bernet. Above, right: A finely incised whalebone ditty box from the latter part of the 19th century has stars of whale ivory set into its wooden top. The Peabody Museum of Salem.

decorate. When a background device, such as a garden, is used to fill up the space on the tooth, it usually does not crowd out the figure but leaves her comfortable looking and self-assured.

Some ambitious carvers attempted to copy ornate illustrations from such publications as *Harper's Weekly* or *Godey's Lady's Book*. This procedure involved pasting the desired illustration onto the tooth, "dotting" it by piercing the outlines of the design through the paper onto the whale ivory with a sharp sailmaker's awl, removing the paper, and connecting the dots to complete the picture. It was no small task, considering the rolling ship, the sun ducking behind the sheets, and the inconvenience of the homemade tools. When the arduous process was successfully completed, the resulting scene was a dense, complicated amalgam of uniformly dark and evenly etched lines. Less skilled workers turned out awkward masses of chunky furrows that could be appreciated only by a wife or mother.

Pornographic fancies also occupied the lonely scrimshander's attention. It is surmised that most of these were buried at sea, but several have survived in various museum collections. The Bedford Whaling Museum, for example, has a much-prized half-clad maiden. Satiric pieces of scrimshaw also are known: one stock piece shows an old tar proposing on bended knee to a maiden whose countenance registers dismay. In another anonymously carved example, the scrim-

shander depicts his hometown lass on one side of a tooth and his "native" love on the other. Between the figures is the inscription "To our wives and sweethearts. May they never meet."

Narrative scenes

The whale hunt itself inspired some of the best examples of the scrimshander's art. A number of fine teeth in various public collections record the whaling scene with the kind of detached, narrative calm experienced by men who have narrowly escaped death. There is a serene control of perspective and subject: waves, whale, ship, whaleboats, and crew are well proportioned and accurate down to the last details of rigging. It seems remarkable that a man who could push an iron lance nine feet into a whale's "life" could wield a three-inch sailmaker's needle with sufficient finesse to produce these carefully drawn scenes.

The narrative decorations on scrimshawed teeth generally are restrained in both subject matter and artistic approach. These understated depictions do not show such dramatic moments as the whale disgorging tons of squid in its death flurry, nor can they possible convey the stench of blubber being "tried out" on deck amidst great heaps of "gunk and gurry." Nor do they generally picture everyday life of the crew in the forecastle. Yet they remain an excellent visual record of the process and tools of whaling.

Baleen work

While the rarest and most prized pieces of scrimshaw are the polished, ornamented teeth, other fine examples were made from the more plentiful whalebone, or baleen. Ship models crafted from baleen, for example, often were made by the captain, who alone dared attempt the exacting task of carving out the replica of his vessel. A superstition of the sea likened the ship to the body of a fair maiden; if the captain's knife slipped while carving his model, the voyage could be jinxed.

Corset busks—long, flexible staves intended to support that ubiquitous feminine undergarment, also were made of baleen. These items expressed the scrimshander's flights of fancy. Geometric patterns etched into the borders of the busk often surround a verse that is intimate or facetious, or both:

> Accept, dear Girl, this busk from me;
> Carved by my humble hand.
> I took it from a Sperm whale's jaw
> One thousand miles from land.
> In many a gale has been the whale
> In which this bone did rest.
> His time is past, his bone at last
> Must now support thy brest.

More than sixty varieties of utilitarian objects carved from baleen are known. Some of the most common are pie crimpers, also known as jagging wheels; swifts, intricate devices used to wind knitting yarn after it is spun; and cane handles "to support our dignity when we are home," as one captain wryly remarked.

An anonymous craft

For the most part New England's scrimshanders did not sign their works. Because the decorated teeth, busks, jaggers, and other objects were regarded as souvenirs with little artistic value, it was not deemed important to affix the maker's name. There are two notable exceptions. Frederick Myrick, who carved an undetermined number of whale teeth on board the ship *Susan*, signed and dated his pieces 1828. Nine of Myrick's teeth from this voyage, including a good likeness of the *Susan*, have been authenticated. Another scrimshander, Edward Burdett, did "portraits" of the ships *William Tell* and *Friends*. Now at the Mystic Seaport Museum, these examples of Burdett's work are notable for their crisp lines and clean design.

A matter of definition

Scholars and collectors do not always agree on what constitutes scrimshaw. Some feel that only ornamental work—that is, pieces with no utilitarian function—deserve the designation. Others would confine the term to those objects, decorated or not, made of whale ivory (teeth), excluding baleen

The aggressive and unpredictable sperm whale caused many a fatality among the intrepid whalers. But their unshakable calm is well expressed in such measured depictions as this one. "S.W." at the base may indicate "sperm whale." The Peabody Museum of Salem.

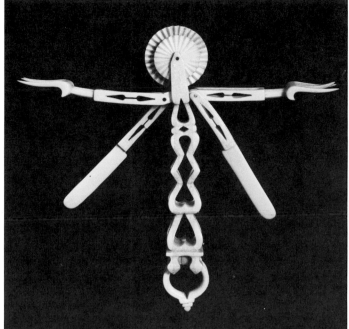

Crimpers like the example at far left were used for cutting pastry. Although this one is carved from a walrus tusk, such tools were often made of whalebone. The ingenious whalebone swift, left, opens like an umbrella to hold a skein of yarn, while it is rolled into a ball. Courtesy Sotheby Parke Bernet.

wares. Dwellers on the island of Nantucket consider scrimshaw to be any object of whale ivory or baleen that is incised with a design; sculptural forms, without etching, are "whalebone carving." Still others feel that "it is scrimshaw if it was made on board ship before 1870."

Fakes and forgeries

Because antique scrimshaw brings higher prices than newly etched pieces, fakery has infiltrated the field. The yellow patina of old ivory has often been imitated by immersing new pieces in oil, tea, or tobacco juice.

An English firm, exporting poor plastic imitations, has duped many unsuspecting buyers. Richard Malley of Mystic Seaport advises, "Look at the incised motifs, and if they resemble 'classics' you have seen before—beware! Put the suspicious specimen under ultraviolet light. True whale ivory will fluoresce, while polymer (the plastic used for faking scrimshaw) will not. Or examine the piece closely with a jeweler's loop. Under this moderate magnification tiny perfectly round air bubbles appear scattered around the ends of the tooth of plastic 'scrimshaw.' Similar holes in real scrimshaw would be irregular in shape." Recent legislation restricting the scrimshaw market (see box) have boosted market prices for antique pieces to near astronomical levels. A pair of teeth attributed to Frederick Myrick of the *Susan*—the last of his pieces to come up at auction—brought $29,000 each. It seems ironic that this traditional seaman's craft, rooted in Yankee notions of thrift (few parts of the whale went to waste), should have become an arena for speculation, despite the fact that interstate sale of whale ivory is not proscribed by law. For those who love the sea, however, scrimshaw teeth, busks, and jaggers will always evoke the spirit of simpler days when sailing ships hunted the great sperm whale. ■

It's a whale of a law

The free spirited, far ranging sperm whale now enjoys the protection of the United States government. The Endangered Species Act of 1973 prohibits interstate commerce of any product derived from endangered species. This applies to scrimshaw made from the teeth of these large mammals, for whom extinction has loomed regrettably near. The United States government does not restrict trade within state boundaries, but permits are usually necessary for scrimshaw commerce within individual states. In 1976, an amendment to the Endangered Species Act exempted from the federal prohibition persons who had owned their scrimshaw before the 1973 act, *if* they applied for and were granted "certificates of exemption." These exemptions were good for three years. In 1979, the exemption permits were extended for three years. What will happen next is uncertain, but it's sure to spark some heated debate between the federal government and those dealers and auction houses who continue to sell antique scrimshaw. A government representative told *Art & Antiques* that a meeting in late February between officials of The Department of the Interior and legal representatives of auction houses and dealers resulted in no further enlightenment concerning applications of the Endangered Species Act. In the meantime, be assured that you *can* legally buy antique scrimshaw—but only within your home state, if its sale is permitted there, or from a dealer or auction house holding an exemption permit.

Painted Tinware

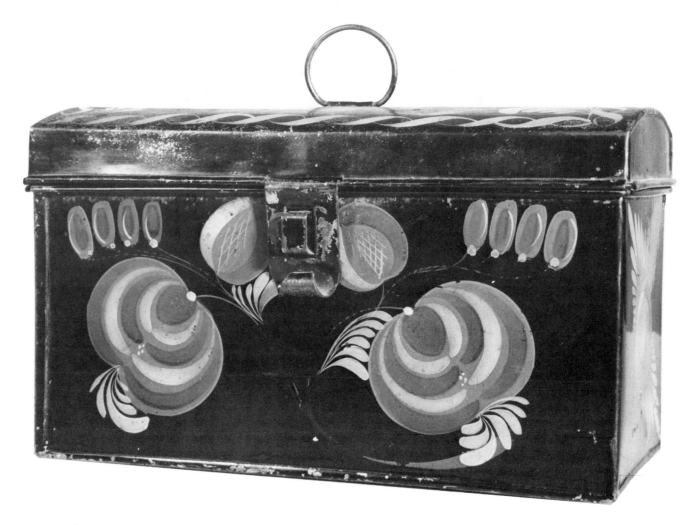

Country tinware—sheet iron or steel coated with tin and painted with colorful floral designs—was peddled in the farms and villages of rural America.

BY MARGARET MATTISON COFFIN

When Charles Messer Stow wrote about Ann Butler's painted tinware in the New York *Sun* in 1933, he started a hunt that is still hotly pursued today. "The best that I have ever seen of American manufacture" and "so strongly individual was her style that it would probably not be difficult to attribute other pieces that may be discovered" were the words the former *Antiques* magazine writer used to describe her wares.

Stow was right: other pieces of Butler-decorated tinware have been discovered, and in the past 50 years a half-dozen amateur detectives have identified tinware from five other shops. This American-decorated tinware, painted freehand in oils and known by modern painters as "country tinware," is colorful, durable, and as cherished today as it was when first sold in the early 1800s. By paying strict attention to a few guidelines noted in the sidebars accompanying this article, you can establish provenance for *some* country tinware both in museum collections and on the antiques market. But first, some background.

The term *tole* is sometimes used as a synonym for American painted tinware. More precisely used, *tole* refers to antique French ironware, which may or may not have been decorated. In the 19th century, when they were first made, such American products were called *japanned ware*, a reference to their lustrous, lacquerlike background varnish. Tinware painters of the 20th century have coined the phrase *country tinware* to identify this ware.

Tinware is made from tinplate, sheet iron, or steel coated with tin. (The first such plating was effected in Europe to keep metal from rusting.) Sheets of plate were imported from Britain until the end of the 19th century and the advent of the McKinley Tariff Act. While tin-rolling mills started production here in the 1830s, supply at the time was limited.

This page and opposite show Connecticut examples. Opposite: Document box attributed to the Filley shop, ca 1850, 5½″ h. Note ball-like forms and cross hatching. Courtesy the late James Stevens. Below: Document box probably from Upson shop, ca 1850, 5″ h. Scalloped white band beneath design and large, simple brush strokes are typical. Left: coffeepot, ca 1830, 9″ h. Shop attribution undetermined; finger painting typical of Connecticut. Both: Smithsonian Institution, Washington, D.C.

CONNECTICUT TINWARE

Connecticut decorators liked painting on white bands, although this is not exclusively a Connecticut device. Asphaltum (japan paint) was the usual background here. *Filley shop* painters produced designs with red balls of various sizes used as the base for both fruits and flowers. In some of these pieces green leaves appear to have been painted with fugitive color, which disappears into the background. There is frequent cross-hatching, sometimes yellow, or white, to highlight these motifs. Every once in a while a simple yellow bird with dark green wings appears in these designs. Brush-stroke borders are strong and simple. Sometimes there are variations of alternating yellow ocher and vermilion

stokes. The tinshop of James Upson and Joseph Cowles started business in Marion, Connecticut, in 1790. Just when a decorating shop was added is not yet known. *Upson shop* painting often features scalloped white bands or other "different" uses of white beneath design. Motifs sometimes appear rather crude because they use just a few overstrokes to give depth. Brushstroke borders are apt to have extra large strokes. Considerable finger blending is found on Upson pieces. More often than not, large flower or fruit motifs are white with vermilion overstrokes or finger blending. (This means of blending color often was adopted by tin painters: they merely pounced their index fingers in wet paint, feathering out one side of a stroke which had been applied with a brush. Often actual fingerprints are obvious.)

This page: Maine examples. Above: Teapot, ca 1820, 5½″ h, attributed to Zachariah Steven's shop, distinctive for imaginative, often asymmetrical designs and use of yellow or olive color leaves. Smithsonian Institution. Right: Document box, ca 1830, 5½″ h. Note thinly painted, white, scalloped border around edge of flowers and the salmon red flowers typical of the Buckley shop. Courtesy Deborah Lambeth. Below: Document box, ca 1840, 6″ h. Another example of Steven's shop work with mixture of flowers and leaves. Courtesy Margaret Emery.

Early manufacture

The first tinware manufactured here was unpainted yet it became popular immediately since it was light, bright, and easy to clean. No one knows the earliest smith to practice his trade in America, but Shem Drowne and other tinplate workers were busy in the Boston-Cambridge area by 1720. The fact that Drowne was a tinsmith suggests that there were others here before him. He was American born, and we have no evidence to indicate that he took his apprenticeship outside this country. Drowne's ledger in the library of the American Antiquarian Society in Worcester, Massachusetts, shows that he made all sorts of common tinware: candle molds and candlesticks, trunks, trays, caddies, funnels, graters, teapots, coffeepots, "spout cups," and sugar bowls. Until the discovery of his ledger, this smith was best known for the copper weathervanes he made, which still survive in the eastern part of Massachusetts. The grasshopper vane atop Faneuil Hall is one example. Although Drowne was identified by his contemporaries as a "tinplate-worker," like others who worked with sheet metals, he fabricated each ware from whatever metal was most appropriate.

There is no evidence that Drowne's tinware was treated with paint or varnish; however, within decades of the time he opened his business, American tinwares were being treated with an asphaltum-base varnish and dried in a kiln: this process was referred to as *japanning*, a term used earlier in Britain. A japan-paint finish was similar *in appearance only* to the finish on furniture which imitated Oriental lacquer. Much antique tinware is protected with this finish; it is often seen on eyeglass cases, undecorated caddies, and spice boxes—common items in today's market. Originally the finish was lustrous and rich looking, usually a coppery brown. It also can be honey colored or black, depending on how much it was thinned with turpentine and the temperature at which it was baked. Once in a while the japan paint was tinted with Prussian blue. Time has dulled old finishes and, since japan paint is brittle, surfaces are often scratched.

By 1810 people began to decorate japanned tinware with country painting—freehand ornamentation using artist's oils thinned in turpentine. (Such painting continued for at least 50 years.) Documents connected with the Oliver Filley tinshop in Bloomfield, Connecticut—a family business, which, in time, sent relatives to open shops in at least five other states—mention both the "flowerers" who painted tin and the painted tinware, itself. In Elizabeth, New Jersey, in 1810, Oliver Filley wrote back to the home shop requesting a shipment of painted ware. Said he: "The inhabitants are making a great parade of Christmas here and tinware sells much better on that account." And Augustus Filley, who left the Connecticut shop a year later to open a store in Lansingburg, New York, ordered trays "with birds on them if you please."

In Filley family letters from 1810–1820 there is also frequent discussion of women decorators, who were in great de-

---

MAINE TINSMITHS

Zachariah Stevens's ornamentation is distinctive. He used combinations of fruits and flowers. Occasionally he painted shells, cornucopias, and baskets in a greater variety of color than usually found on country tin. Some fruits and flowers are quite realistic; others—flowers, especially—are highly imaginative and not made up merely of brushstroke petals. The blending with a brush of wet oil paints of different colors makes Stevens's painting look different from other country painting, most of which was done using wet-on-dry paint. The leaves he painted were usually in shades of olive green and yellow. Done without veins, their shapes are quite consistent—simple, rather fat ovoids with pointed ends. Borders on these pieces are more imaginative than those found on any other country tinware.

Like the others, *Buckley tinware* trays, caddies, and such are painted with recognizable characteristics. Designs are often symmetric and sometimes, especially on document boxes, are made up of a series of borders in red, green, and yellow. Buckley flowers sometimes have brushstroke petals. Quite often, round, salmon-colored balls make up a part of a flower; frequently there are heavy white overstrokes on these and sometimes parts of motifs appear to have a thin black wash over them. The paint that tinted the wash was probably a fugitive color (perhaps green) that changed over the years. Some flowers have thin scallops of white around their edges. Centers of flowers, like those Stevens did, often are cross-hatched with delicate lines. Leaves may be either green or yellow brushstrokes, or heart shaped, with fat center veins and fine outer ones. Another favorite leaf is green with a yellow vein down one side and straight finer veins extending from it. The Buckleys sometimes used red bands beneath borders. Another favorite design for the front of a trunk is a single drape, starting high on one side, dipping to the bottom of the trunk in the center and finishing again in an upper corner.

Background colors used in Maine vary: artists most commonly used black japan, but you also see red, yellow, and white paint. The less usual colors came from the Stevens's shop.

NEW YORK TIN

In New York State a variety of painted patterns are found in the vicinity where the *Filley shop's* peddlers from Lansingburg traveled. Some tinware from the area features orange-vermillion flowers and fruits with fine black details, all on a white band. There is finger blending on these motifs, usually yellow on the orangy color. Many trunks with these designs have distinctive decoration on the lids—motifs made up of multiple brushstrokes applied expertly in graduated sizes. There are also trunks with rather simple red-green motifs on white bands plus a spray of flowers and leaves beneath on the front of the trunk. A type of ornamentation with sprays of flowers going from lower left to upper right also appears to have been done in the Lansingburg shop. These patterns are in vermillion, cadmium yellow, and green; stems are often red. A close relative of this pattern has a similar spray with wet-on-wet painting on the flowers or fruits, Prussian blue on white or vice versa. The green is a dark blue-green, the red a bright vermilion; white brushstrokes replace the usual yellow. Stripes and bands are patriotic combinations of red, white, and blue. Some of this last-described painting is crude, as if the painter were a novice or working too fast.

Some pieces attributed to the *North shop* have a series of borders in red, green, and yellow brushstrokes. Red and green bands as well as white were used beneath borders. The largest brushstrokes in motifs were apt to have clusters of dots on the large end of the stroke. Many green brushstrokes have yellow stripes along one side. Clusters of brushstrokes making up motifs on the tops of trunks, for example, are red, green, and yellow. Another type of design popular on trunks and attributed to the North shop has an ovoid red flower in the center with brushstroke petals; leaves and decorative brushstrokes curve outward toward the corners. Painting identified as North is skillfully executed. Background paint on this tinware is japan paint, often mottled by brush marks in a regular pattern made with darker paint.

Butler tinware also featured white bands and used tiny red brushstroke flowers; blue, starlike blossoms; and small leaves with scalloped edges. Clusters of dots make little flowers. The allover effect of a Butler piece is often busy. Sometimes the Butlers used colorful baskets. Their designs are carefully balanced and stems are unusually thin. Elongated tulips and fat rose buds are favorite flowers. Overstrokes of white and alizarin are exceptionally slender. Leaves are ovoid with veins and outlines in pale yellow. Borders are yellow exclusively. Sometimes their green leans toward emerald. Rickrack and rope borders are used. The Butlers painted many bread and bun trays with quick, simple almost geometric motifs. These are referred to as their "commercial" wares. The Butler women signed some of their work, probably gifts to family members. Initials and complete names have been found. Sometimes Ann enclosed her initials within a heart. One extra-fancy trunk has "Ann Butler, Greenville, N.Y." inscribed on the bottom. The background paint on Butler ware was usually dark japan paint.

Top right: Trunk, ca 1850, 9″ h, from New York's Butler shop showing Ann's signature on the bottom. The Butler women signed some of their work, usually gifts. On the right side of this box note the rather busy but beautifully painted design filling the whole space and, along the top edge, a star-like border—all characteristics typical of the shop. Private Collection. Above left and right: Apple tray, 1800-1850, 11″ square, and document box, ca 1820, 6″ h, both attributed to Filley shop. The use of vermillion on the box and the use of multiple brush strokes applied in graduating sizes on the tray are typical, as are the fine black line details painted in the fruits on the box. Courtesy The Henry Ford Museum and author's collection (photo by Charles Coffin), respectively.

mand as tinware painters and who went from shop to shop to work. Very often women in a tinsmith's family painted while men made and peddled the ware. Decorating was not exclusively women's work though: Oliver Filley, Harvey Filley (who started a tinware shop in Philadelphia in about 1820), Edward Francis, and Zachariah Stevens were all known tinware painters. Considerable country tinware was produced in Connecticut, where there were many early tinshops in addition to the Filley shop; among the best known were those of the Pattisons—perhaps the first tinsmiths in Connecticut—the Upsons, the Norths, and the Filleys. These shops trained apprentices and sent out peddlers to sell or trade tinware, especially in rural areas.

Several Maine families also are associated with painted tinware. The Zachariah Stevens family is the best known. Zachariah was the great-great-grandfather of the late Esther Stevens Brazer, one of the first authorities on early painted tinware, painted furniture, and decorated walls. Born in 1778

in Stevens Plains just west of Portland, Zachariah grew up, married, and lived there throughout his lifetime. Family records, however, mark a short interlude spent in the Boston-Cambridge area, and perhaps this was where he learned his trade. His tinshop opened in 1798 and by the 1830s Zachariah's sons, Samuel and Alfred, were managing the shop. It burned in 1842 and was not rebuilt. Considerable tinware painted by the elder Stevens or those he taught has been found, thanks to Brazer's identification of family pieces.

A second type of decoration found in Stevens Plains, Maine, is identified as "Buckley." Oliver Buckley was born in Connecticut in 1781 and migrated to Maine in time to set up a tinshop there in the early 1800s. (He purchased land from the Stevenses in 1807 and was advertising tinplate working in a Portland newspaper eight years later.) A whole category of tin painting has been attributed to the Buckley shop based on a Brazer finding. She discovered a trunk with the scratched initials M.A.B., a monogram which could stand for Mary Ann

This page and opposite: Pennsylvania examples. Top: Octagonal tray, ca 1850, 12½" long, with characteristic crystallized bottom. Smithsonian Institution. Far right: Coffeepot, ca 1850, 12" h, with bold design, accented with elaborate fine, black lines. Winterthur Museum. Right: Candle holder, ca 1850, 6½" dia., also has typical fine black lines in design. Winterthur. Opposite, left: Bread tray, 1800-1850, 12" long. Winterthur. Opposite, right: Octagonal tray, ca 1850, 12" long, with crystallized bottom. Hitchcock Museum, Riverton, Connecticut.

Buckley, one of Oliver's daughters. It is not important whether the tinware was painted by a Buckley; the ware is found in quantities in Maine and the assumed association provides a means of classifying another series of tin-painting designs.

Some tinware shapes are indigenous to Maine. One is a flat-topped trunk. Another is a trunk whose lid has a platform raised on curved pieces of tinplate which form beveled joints.

The Fly Creek Shop of Stephen North, above Cooperstown, New York, produced painted tin as well. A bread tray at the New York Historical Association with a faint "Mercy North" written on its base started the search for the North shop in the 1950s. Stephen had brought his family west from Connecticut after he learned his trade; the shop opened its doors sometime between 1800 and 1810. Stephen managed it for years and eventually Alfred and Linus, his two older sons, also became tinsmiths. One of Stephen's daughters, Mercy, undoubtedly learned decorating and it is assumed that North girls from Connecticut, visiting their Fly Creek cousins, taught the New Yorkers the craft.

Ann Butler's tinware and that of the Butler family first publicized by Charles Messer Stow originated in the Catskill Mountain farm community near Greenville, New York called Brandy Hill. The father, Aaron, was a tinsmith; daughters Ann, Minerva, and Marilla, at least, were painters. It appears that no decorators outside of the family were hired, and the decoration the women used is easily recognized.

Identifying painted Pennsylvania tinware has been a challenge. The collections of country tin in Pennsylvania museums are among the best anywhere, but it seems as if researchers have been able to do little more than point out the kinds of decoration that probably came out of the Filley shop in Philadelphia and the kinds of ware that seem to be *found* consistently in William Penn's fair state. The problem is complicated further by our knowledge that decorators, as well as tinsmiths and japanners, went from shop to shop: correspondence between Filleys proves that this exchange occurred between their Philadelphia, Lansingburg, and Bloomfield shops. Perhaps shape can help a little in identifying Pennsylvania pieces: there seem to be more hooked-spout coffeepots found in Pennsylvania than elsewhere, although we know that some were made in Connecticut by Oliver Brunson and undoubtedly by smiths in other states.

Identifying the tinware's decorator

You should not assume that a name found on tinware necessarily denotes a decorator. Interpreting the names that appear is often surprisingly tricky because only rarely do they lead to a tinshop or a decorator. Butler and North signatures are happy exceptions. When names or initials were painted in a prominent place, they identified the owner, as in instances where they are scratched in the raw tin on the underside of the lid of a trunk. A name painted on the bottom or back of tinware may well indicate the painter. Occasionally a ped-

dler scratched his name in the japan paint on the bottom of a country-tin item; if this was the case, figures representing price or size often accompany the name. At other times a whole series of names, perhaps with places and dates, was scratched on the underside of a tray or a trunk lid. These lists suggest a kind of family register. Here are a few typical inscriptions:

SUBMIT FLETCHER (painted on front of trunk)

PHEBE HOLT (painted on back of trunk); *PHEBE THOMSON JULY 1819* (scratched on bottom of same trunk)

HANNAH B. STANTON Touch not this trunk/for fear of shame For here you see/the owner's name; NORWICH, CONN. FEB. THE 28th 1835

C.C. SPENCER #5 (scratched on the bottom of a trunk)

FRANCIS B. RICHARDSON'S CREAM JUG (painted on bottom)

Tinware distribution

Some country tinware was sold directly from tinshops, and a fair amount probably went to country stores. P. T. Barnum, in *The Life of P. T. Barnum*, reports that when he was a young store clerk, he arranged a lottery to get rid of an overstock of tinware growing old and dusty on store shelves. But much country tin was distributed and bartered from the back of peddlers' wagons. Every housewife had something he wanted—a pound of sheep's fleece "unwashed but free from manure;" dried raspberries or blackberries; half-a-dozen pairs of knitted socks; some tea leaves; goose feathers or a bit of handwoven, part-linen tow cloth. She might trade these things for a gay piece of tinware to brighten her table or shelf.

Tin peddlers were often robbed and murdered because they had a reputation for carrying cash in secret money belts worn under their clothing next to their hearts. There were many legends told about them. Tinsmiths' ghostly spirits sat in cellar corners midst their rusting wares, or their tin carts rattled down roads on moonless nights to disappear in mist. In a similar story, a kitchen floor is eternally stained with a peddler's blood despite daily scrubbings. And a ghostly itinerant, decapitated by robbers, searches for his head along a lonely roadway in Vermont.

The ghosts of peddlers, tinplate workers, and tin painters of the past remain with us. As we look toward the future, we anticipate learning more about them, hoping to identify additional painters like tinsmith-painter Zachariah Stevens and the decorator who used a heart inscription, Ann Butler.■

PENNSYLVANIA TINWARE

Painted coffeepots found in Pennsylvania are apt to have a wide band at the base, perhaps scalloped, and a narrower band at the top. Brushstroke borders on these bands often have alternating colored strokes: red–green–red–green. Flowers and fruits on white bands or circles are bold. Tulips are popular and different from those of the Butlers or Stevens Plains painters—bigger, brighter, and accented with fine black details. White bands are found on trunks, trays, and caddies as well as on coffeepots. Finger blending of paint is frequent. A motif used sometimes on a red background is an oval fruit shape of gray with black and white overstrokes. Also in evidence is a flower and leaf motif all in yellow with fine black detail, frequently combined with a type of ornamentation already described, the yellow motif used, for instance, on the ends of a bread tray or the bottom border of a coffeepot. Although, as usual, japan paint is the common background, red is found often enough to imply that it was used deliberately to attract the Pennsylvania German housewife. Flash crystallized backgrounds are also found more frequently in Pennsylvania than in other states. To crystallize, tinplate was treated with an acid which marked the metal in crystal-like patterns. Such tinplate, when manufactured into a tray, was covered only with a thin coat of varnish so that the sparkling designs showed through.

Salt-Glazed Stoneware

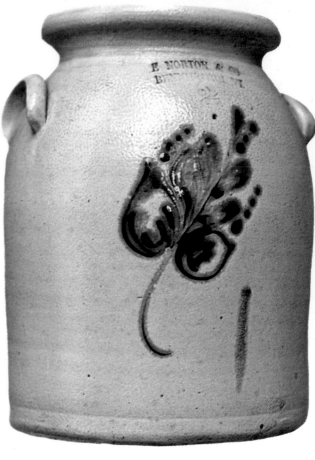

Salt-glazed stoneware was common to every 19th-century American household, shop, and tavern. Today, these ceramic vessels remain popular among collectors because of their unique vitality and the charm of their free-flowing motifs.

BY RUTH AMDUR TANENHAUS

Salt-glazed stoneware pottery was an indispensable item in 19th-century America. Unlike its contemporary mass-produced counterpart, each piece of stoneware was hand-formed and, more often than not, hand-decorated with popular folk-art motifs, including graceful flowers, bold eagles, pecking chickens, and stylized log cabins. These containers, produced in numerous forms and sizes, were used in the kitchen, dairy, tavern, and shop for storage, salting, and pickling. Jugs, crocks, jars, and bottles were designed to sell at low prices and were decorated intially by pictorial incising and later by glaze painting. Although decoration was subordinate to function and the pottery was not considered a high art form in its day, it is currently enjoying a surge in popularity and is recognized and collected as an example of simple but charming folk art.

Origins

Although adapted for 19th-century commercial requirements, North American salt-glazed stoneware was a derivative of earlier European forms and techniques. Stoneware was known in Europe from the Middle Ages on, when Arab caravans traded with China. It is thought that by the 13th century German potters were making basic stoneware vessels. Instead of emulating the Chinese colored glazes, however, the Germans eventually developed a method of salt-glazing in which common salt, vaporized in the intense heat of the kiln, combined chemically with silica in the pottery to form an impervious and inert transparent glaze. Rhenish stoneware containers of the 17th and 18th centuries were sold extensively to England and, in turn, to the American colonies. Typically in the form of mugs, tankards, jars, and chamber pots, Rhenish vessels often were decorated with elements in molded relief, such as foliage, masks, and heraldic seals. Elaborate incised work was also frequent and sometimes was combined with blue glazing. These wares ultimately served as models to the native American stoneware potter.

Two prominent early 18th-century stoneware potteries preceded the spread of the industry throughout the colonies. One, established by William Rogers at Yorktown, Virginia, operated during the 1720s and 1730s. Excavated examples show that Rogers's pieces followed the English style in both form and technique, patterned after brown-glazed work, and included mugs, tankards, pots, bowls, and jugs. The other early stoneware pottery was Andrew Duché's; he operated in Philadelphia during the same period. The Duché pieces were of a different tradition than those of the English style, and similar to Rhenish work. They were characterized by gray bodies and ornamented with blue cobalt-oxide glaze.

What became the characteristic style of North American stoneware was an adaptation of Rhenish blue-decorated and gray-bodied ware. In the earlier phase, the late 18th to early 19th centuries, American stoneware was quite similar to the Rhenish types, in vessel shapes, incised and blue-filled decoration, and productive methods. The evolution to indigenous

Below: Wide-mouth crock, Riedinger and Caire, Poughkeepsie, New York. Surface glazed with bluebird in cobalt. Opposite: Water cooler, E. Norton and Company, Bennington, Vermont. Both: Collection of Mr. and Mrs. Lewis Smith; photos by Thomas S. Berntsen.

Early American stoneware potters utilized incised and blue-filled decoration; but after 1850, incised designs gave way to the faster process of surface painting with sweeping blue slip designs. Right: Water or cider jug, ca 1868, Hubbel & Chesebro, Geddes, New York. The name of the pottery is stamped above the design. Note the bunghole, reinforced by four equidistant screws, at bottom front. The National Gallery of Art, Index of American Design. Below: View of a water jug, 1798, Clarkson Crolius, New York City. Here the conventional decoration was incised and filled in with blue glaze. The New-York Historical Society, Elie Nadelman Collection; photo the National Gallery of Art, Index of American Design.

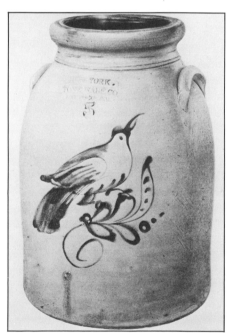

"Stoneware was hard and dense, incapable of absorbing water, and unlikely to chip."

American forms and decorative styles was a result of the different American environment and culture and, especially with later pieces, of the influence of a progressive machine technology. Eventually, then, there developed a unique North American ceramic style. These wares were produced in profusion first in the Northeast and then in the Midwest; stoneware pottery was less common in the Southeast, and the few vessels of this region were virtually devoid of decoration.

An important distinction exists between stoneware and earthenware. Earthenware, composed of common clay and produced by a simple process, was the medium for much American utilitarian pottery. The completed piece was porous and required a glaze to make it watertight. But the glaze most common to American household pottery contained lead, a substance pernicious to both craftsman and consumer. The *Pennsylvania Mercury* of 1785 contained the following admonition:

> The best of Lead-glazing is esteemed unwholsome, by observing people. The Mischievous effects of it, fall chiefly on the country people, and the poor every where. Even when it is firm enough, so as not to scale off, it yet is imperceptibly eaten away by every acid matter; and mixing with the drinks and meats of the people, becomes a slow but sure poison, chiefly affecting the nerves, that enfeebles the constitution, and produces paleness, tremors, gripes, palsies etc. sometimes to whole families.

This danger did not exist with stoneware. Fired to much greater temperatures, it was hard and dense, incapable of absorbing water, and unlikely to chip. The stoneware vessels were glazed to produce a smooth surface, esthetically appealing and easily cleaned. And instead of utilizing toxic lead to produce a glaze, the glaze was achieved by what the *Pennsylvania Mercury* termed "the most perfect and wholesome glazing, produced only from Sand and Salts."

The basic difficulty in establishing a stoneware industry was obtaining the special type of body clay, which was unavailable in most areas of the United States. Practically every stoneware pottery in New England and New York imported its clay from either South Amboy, New Jersey, the source of the best variety, or from Long Island, where the quality was just a bit lower. The most prominent and productive potteries were located close to water routes. The potteries of Bennington, Albany, Fort Edward, and Troy, for example, were near the Hudson River; thus raw clay from New Jersey was easily transported, and the finished wares, in turn, were distributed at points along the water routes. By the

1820s new canal systems, in particular the Erie Canal and its tributaries, made stoneware factories practicable in more remote locations, as clay could be loaded onto large canal boats at South Amboy and transported throughout New York State and the regions of the Great Lakes.

The price lists and order forms of the era provide interesting insight into America's simpler and less costly past. For example, in 1837 the respected Clark Pottery in Athens, New York, priced four-gallon pots and jugs at $.54 each, or $6.48 a dozen. By 1852 the Nortons in Bennington listed the same goods at only $8.00 a dozen.

Fabrication

After several weeks in transit the clay arrived at its destination—raw, unpurified, and almost dry. A machine called a pug mill restored the clay to a plastic state and prepared it for the potter's wheel. The pug mill, acting like a slow beater or mixer, and turned by horse or water power, broke up and mixed the dry clay with water and sand. The cylindrical machine was then emptied from the bottom, and the semifluid clay was worked through screens to remove stones and hard lumps.

The plastic clay was then presented to the thrower, whose job was to form jars, crocks, jugs, and bottles. Turning the base of the potter's wheel with his feet, the craftsman first centered the lump of clay, then hollowed out the lump as the wheel turned rapidly. Using wet hands and wooden tools, he shaped and raised the walls of the piece and then formed a rim or narrowed the top to form the neck of a jug. This procedure took only several minutes, and the thrower had to be both accomplished and fast, as he frequently formed several hundred pieces a day.

The majority of stoneware pieces required handles. In the 19th century, handles were extruded by forcing clay from an opening at one end of a tube, similar to a baker's pastry tube. The clay rope was then cut to a specific length and hand-pressed onto the finished vessel. A final smoothing with a damp cloth and the pot was then left to dry, with only five minutes having passed since it began as an amorphous clay lump. The still-wet clay was impressed with a hand stamp stating the name of the pottery or the major purchaser.

Most potteries dried their pieces at low temperatures in wood-fired drying ovens. It generally took one to three days for the plastic clay to dry into greenware—dry, unfired clay that was fragile and brittle. It was then washed inside with a slip, a fine clay mixed in a solution until liquid. Albany slip, the most common, a brown or black clay mined from the Hudson River, was used to line the insides of most North American stoneware after 1805.

Once the clay had dried, it was ready for decorative incising or glaze painting. And once decorated, the pieces were ready for firing.

In addition to food containers, potters
created more unusual objects. Above:
Teapot, 1780-1825. An early, rare piece.
Below: Figure of dog, 1800-1875,
possibly by Daniel Boughner of
Greensboro, Pennsylvania. Potters often
amused their children with animals
made from leftover clay ("whimsies").
Right: Water cooler, 1853, probably by
T.W. Whiteman, Perth Amboy, New
Jersey. Note the applied, raised
medallion. All, Winterthur Museum.

Stoneware required a temperature of approximately 2,300 degrees Fahrenheit to turn the clay-sand mixture into a hard, dense ceramic. The procedure was carried out in a large, brick-lined, thick-walled, earth-covered, wood-burning kiln. The process took from six to eight days. The labor costs of this operation were high, as the kiln had to be checked and refueled day and night. Thus the kiln was loaded to accommodate as many pieces as possible—from several hundred to 1,000 wares at a firing.

As only the outsides were to be salt-glazed, the greenware—or dried but unfired ware—was stacked in columns, sometimes six to eight pieces high, resting on setting tiles. Because the typical vessel shapes were based on the cone and cylinder and thus had their own structural strength, the pieces on the bottom levels generally endured the weight from above. To make the vertical columns more stable, pieces of raw clay known variously as cockspurs, wedges, or saggers were inserted between the pots.

When the kiln was fully loaded and closed, a fire was started underneath. The temperature was raised gradually so that the pottery would not crack. Eventually, after perhaps two days, the temperature reached the maximum of 2,200 to 2,300 degrees, and the pottery was ready for salt-glazing. The top of the kiln was opened and the glazers shoveled roughly a bushel of common rock salt inside then quickly closed the kiln opening. When the salt was subjected to the intense heat, it vaporized immediately and combined with and covered all the exposed surfaces. The resulting glaze was not just a layer of condensed salt; the vaporized sodium combined with the silica in the stoneware to form a hard glassy surface of sodium silicate.

After the salt-glazing process was completed, the high temperature was maintained for three to four more days. This assured the fusion of the pieces. Then the temperature was slowly lowered. The kiln was cooled as slowly and evenly as it had been heated. Finally, the kiln was opened and the stoneware was removed. The entire process took approximately seven to ten days.

Decoration

Although the stoneware vessels from the early part of the 19th century boast varied and subtle shapes, the lasting appeal of this pottery form is more the result of the decorative motifs, which were inspired by the American environment. The images were either incised in the wet clay or, later, glaze-painted in blue on the dried greenware.

The stoneware decorators were not trained artists. As Donald Webster notes in his definitive work, *Decorated Stoneware Pottery of North America* (Charles E. Tuttle Co., 1971), the decorators were merely adding sales appeal to these functional vessels. The pottery was not a crafts outlet but rather a small manufacturing operation. These individuals had little education or training, were untraveled, and were the products of limited environments—"folk" artists on all counts. Their designs reflect a strong sense of nationalism, evidenced by the eagles, flags, and warships, and an enjoyment of nature, reflected in the flora and fauna. Simple flower and leaf decorations required minimal work, were universally appealing, and accounted for more designs than all other decorative themes combined.

Decorators used three basic techniques: impressing with a stamp in the plastic clay, incising in semidried clay, and surface glazing, executed with a brush or slip-cup quill on dried but unfired greenware.

Incising involved cutting the outlines of a design into the soft pot. When dry, the lines frequently were filled with a blue glaze. It was a most time-consuming procedure, as control was needed over the placement of the lines as well as over the depth and width of each. Uneven application of pressure could result in an inferior effect. Thus, by the 1840s, as the stoneware industry grew and the objective was to produce pots in great quantity, this incising technique was halted.

Impressing or stamping was basically a mechanical process. Relief stamps, bearing the maker's name and other designs, were pressed into the wet clay and left an impression that resembled neat incising. If the stamped motif required coloration, the stamp was dipped into blue glaze before each application to the clay body. Stamped designs occasionally were combined with hand-incising, but as the century advanced the incising method declined, as did the decorative stamping. However, stamps continued to be used to denote names of potteries.

From 1850 on, the decorative technique was glaze painting, accomplished with either a brush or slip cup. The slip cup was a small ceramic vessel with an opening on top. It stored the glaze. A porcupine quill projected from a small hole in front. Brush glazing and quill tracing were much faster than incising, and elaborate designs were applied to most pieces. Extravagant and large-scale pictures—occasionally covering entire sides of what were essentially storage jugs—became popular, imparting character and appeal.

The shapes of the stoneware vessels initially were influenced by European antecedents and by the classical revival from the 1790s to the 1840s. Ovoid forms and cyma curves were common. The pieces had small bases and top-heavy bodies. Although visually striking, these vessels, once filled

with liquid, were rather unstable. The classic forms yielded necessarily to more utilitarian and easily formed shapes. Bases became wider and thus more stable, the side curves flatter, and the rims heavier and hence less fragile. By 1860 the basic stoneware shape was the cylinder with straight sides and thick rims.

Uses for stoneware

Stoneware vessels had many uses: jugs held cider, beer, whiskey, vinegar, oil, and molasses. Butter churns and batter jugs were numerous, and jars were used for salting meat, pickling, and preserving foods. Tradesmen used stoneware jars to transport turpentine and acids. Merchants stored goods in stoneware and often gave the container along with the stock to the customer. In taverns, stoneware mugs, coolers, bottles, and jugs were used for storing and drinking.

Prominent potteries

Successful continuation of the more prominent stoneware potteries was due, in large measure, to the strength of the

Opposite page: Jug, 1844, probably from Pennsylvania. The stylized bird-and-flower design is incised and painted with blue slip. A vine circles the shoulder, and the twin handles are decorated with splashes of glaze. The National Gallery of Art, Index of American Design. Above: Water or beer pitcher, ca 1850, Williams and Carl Wingender Pottery, Haddonfield, New Jersey. The National Gallery of Art, Index of American Design. Left: Flower pot, 1820-1850, possibly from New England. Around the outside of the pot is a very unusual, applied, low relief, molded decoration of various forms. The Winterthur Museum.

family ties, to the direct participation from generation to generation in the maintenance of the operation. A case in point is the Bennington Pottery that operated for 101 years. It was founded by Capt. John Norton in 1793. He took his two sons, Luman and John, into partnership with him around 1815, before his own retirement from the establishment in 1823. In 1833 Luman Norton in turn took his son Julius into the business. And in 1845 Julius Norton took his brother-in-law, Christopher Webber Fenton, into partnership with him. The story continues as additional offspring were involved in the pottery. For over a century, then, the Norton family controlled this distinguished pottery, with no record of any form of labor trouble.

The White family in Utica, New York, ran another well-managed pottery whose signature became the bird and flower designs on their crocks and jugs. By the time the establishment closed in 1906, White's pottery had grown to be among the largest New York State stoneware potteries, selling wares throughout the state, New England, and California. The success of the White pottery can be attributed to its capable handling by Noah White and his son Nicholas. Its history is again one of steady growth and continued family management. The firm even had an off-shoot in Binghamton, New York, when Noah White's daughter and her husband, William

Roberts, a potter employed by her father, moved to Binghamton in 1848. The Binghamton operation remained in business for nearly a quarter of a century.

Effects of technology

Technological and industrial advance, however, ultimately doomed the stoneware pottery industry. By the late 1860s there was safe vacuum canning in glass jars; the 1870s saw the introduction of ice refrigerators and refrigerated transport of meats. And by the 1880s, mass-molded, inexpensive glass of many varieties was abundant. So the need for these relatively bulky, heavy vessels declined, and by 1910 the salt-glazed stoneware industry had ceased to exist.

Salt-glazed stoneware was common to every 19th-century household, shop, and tavern. Essential objects, the vessels changed only slightly during the century. As a medium of folk art, the pottery generally lacks superb esthetic refinement. Yet it has a unique flavor, imagery, and vitality. It harks back to rural America, to a less complex and more self-sufficient society. It is perhaps this nostalgia for a vanished era, coupled with the charm of the simple free-flowing motifs, that has made stoneware vessels so popular and collectible, and has allowed this utilitarian craft finally to assume its proper place in the ceramic history of the United States. ■

Mochaware

Despite its evocative name, mochaware encompasses several varieties of slip-glazed pottery, decorated with a number of distinctive motifs—not all of them brown.

BY RUFUS FOSHEE

Although mochaware is enthusiastically collected in both the United States and in England, where much of it was made during the late 18th and the 19th centuries, there has been no general agreement on a precise yet all-encompassing definition for this type of pottery. The name itself is both deceptive and limiting, suggesting a ware that is either brown in body (most mocha in fact has a cream-colored or yellow pottery base) or one that is decorated in this characteristic color. In reality, mochaware occurs in many distinctive variations.

The term mochaware was first coined not with reference to the familiar beverage, but rather to suggest the visual similarity between the seaweedlike slip decoration on some early wares and mocha stone—a type of English agate with mossy green or red striations.

Writing in *The Magazine Antiques* in 1945, Robert J. Sim suggested that a more appropriate name for early mocha might be "banded creamware," because prior to 1830 most mochaware consisted of a creamware of pottery body encircled with slip-glaze bands of distinctive decorative motifs. In the same publication in 1966, Susan Van Rensselaer seemed to support that terminology, noting, however, that all

examples of mochaware did not have creamware bodies. The possibility of agreement on an all-encompassing definition was rendered still more remote when scholar Geoffrey Godden, writing in *British Pottery—An Illustrated Guide* (1965), identified mocha pottery as only those wares decorated with a brown seaweed motif achieved through the application of "tea" made from turpentine, tobacco juice, and urine.

A broader definition is clearly needed.

One of the problems in defining mochaware has been the tendency of some writers to assume that it was all made from a single, particular type of clay body—a notion that is still prevalent among collectors. It would be more accurate to define mochaware in terms of its decoration—which is distinctive and, in its many variations, recognizable even to the novice collector.

Most examples of mocha-type decoration made before 1830, are found on creamware—a light-bodied English earthenware covered with a tin slip glaze—or pearlware, creamware with cobalt added to the glaze for whiteness. (Some of the very earliest and rarest pieces of mocha, however, have plain earthenware bodies of a less delicate hue than creamware, and an ocher-colored underglaze.) When pearlware went out of fashion around 1830, mocha decoration was applied to yellow ware—a type of earthenware underglazed in a yellow slip varying from a warm pumpkin to a dull tan color, with a clear overglaze.

While nearly all creamware and pearlware were made in

England, some yellow ware was made in the United States as well, throughout the 19th century and into the 20th. Although it is difficult for a novice to distinguish between American-made and British-made mochaware, the experienced collector can detect characteristic details of potting, glazing, and coloring in the English examples. However, because there are relatively few American examples known, there is not a sound basis for comparison. English mochaware is, for all intents and purposes, "all that counts." Although mocha was made by many individual factories over a relatively long period of time, it is extremely rare to find a piece bearing a maker's mark.

Decoration: the distinguishing factor

Again, it is important to remember that mochaware cannot be identified purely by association with a particular type of body ware. It is the type of decoration used on these bodies that ultimately distinguishes a piece of mocha from another kind of ware. The diversity of decoration within the mocha

generic, however, is great; its range is unmatched by any other type of British ceramic made between 1750 and 1875.

The surface of mochaware has a buildup of slip decoration which is easily felt by rubbing the surface. There is usually a base coat of white or colored slip glaze, topped with one of the more distinctive motifs arranged within glaze bands of contrasting color. There may be as many as 26 of these decorative bands on a large piece such as a jug. The bands may vary in width. Some pieces have a single band of glaze several inches wide, upon which other decorative slipglaze motifs are applied. Other pieces may have two dozen narrow bands

Above: a representative selection of mochaware displaying the wide range of decoration applied from about 1750 to 1875. The different clay bodies seen here include creamware, yellow ware and stoneware; most pieces have characteristic applied bands. Counting from left to right, top to bottom, numbers 2, 6 and 8 show a cat's eye motif; number 10, earthworm; and numbers 3, 4, 5, 7, 12, and 14, variations on the seaweed theme. Courtesy Inez French, Marta Larson, Joan Foshee. Photo Ben Margo. Opposite: Pitcher, Historic Deerfield, Inc.; Deerfield, Massachusetts.

of plain glaze combined with one or more wide bands upon which other designs are painted. And some mochaware is plainly decorated with simple unornamented bands of colored glaze.

The range of color on mochaware is usually subtle, with banding and other slip decoration often found in shades of blue or grey, as well as brown, green, and ocher. Blue and white decoration is sometimes seen alone.

Mochaware patterns

Mochaware motifs readily recognized by experienced collectors include the seaweed, the earthworm, the cat's eye, and the marble or tortoiseshell design. The seaweed motif resembles fronds of swaying, fernlike vegetation. It may occur in blue, green, or black colors as well as the expected brown or "tea" shades. The earthworm motif may flow along in a fairly straight banding around a mug or a jug, or it may swirl in great loops, losing the visual sense of a true earthworm, but creating a charming design.

The cat's eye pattern has many variations. Sometimes the cat's eyes resemble oysters but most often they are round orbs. Two of the most complex mochaware designs—and these are encountered with frequency—are intended to mimic marble and tortoiseshell. Sometimes these motifs are called "agate" because of their typical striations.

Two very pleasing but not often encountered mochaware patterns have related white glaze motifs. In the first, simple, connected white circles appear on a rather dark ground; in the second, wavy white lines of slip are vertically arranged or intertwined to create a gridlike design. Such patterns have been called "comb" designs, but they should not be confused with combware—an entirely different genre of pottery having a red body and comblike designs scratched into its surface, rather than painted on.

There is also an atypical mochaware banded with textured, sandlike areas that cover a good part of the body surface of a hollow piece. Such examples are not only sand textured but usually sand colored, with bands of blue or brown above and below the central rough-surfaced area.

Typical mochaware forms

Mocha decoration has been found on a wide variety of forms, most of them hollow pieces. Mugs and bowls are most common, but mustard pots, teapots, shakers, jugs, and beakers are also known. Flat pieces like plates and saucers are extremely rare.

Condition

Competition for pieces of mochaware in mint condition is fierce among experienced collectors. It is much easier to find pieces in "fair to good" but not mint condition, owing to the relative softness of the ware. One of the special joys of collecting mochaware is finding a rare piece of unusual color, form, or decoration. The finest, early examples embody the ultimate in the development of creamware and pearlware, the mature fruits of late 18th-century English ceramic art. ■

The creamer and sugar bowl at left, from a private collection, display a late-19th century decorative variation: wide textured bands of a gritty or sand-like substance. Mugs, like the three shown below, are perhaps the most common mochaware form; these, however, are early examples. On its wide center band, the mug at the left combines the cat's eye, earthworm, and seashell motifs. The center mug, banded at top and bottom, is decorated with marbelized or "end paper" slip; the mug at the right is a fine example of tortoiseshell decoration. Historic Deerfield, Inc., Deerfield, Massachusetts. The mustard pot at the bottom of this page is a very rare form. On a creamware base, it displays a wide central band embellished with the earthworm motif. Private collection.

Opposite page: Both pieces are decorated with variations of the seaweed motif. The mug at right is a rare marked example of mochaware stamped on the base *M Clark 1799*. Ipswich Museum, England.

Cantonware

C hina's great trading port lent its name to an entire category of porcelain wares exported to the western market.

BY SUSAN E. MEYER

As the *Empress of China* sailed into the Port of Canton in 1784, the men on board must have experienced an overwhelming surge of pride. This was indeed a triumphant moment: the first vessel to sail into China under an American flag! The victory had not been won easily. After all, it was precisely the issue of trade that had helped to precipitate the American Revolution. Eleven years before, the American colonists had expressed their objection to the monopoly on trade held by the British East India Company by dumping a load of steeply taxed tea into the Boston Harbor. Immediately after the last battle was won—the ink still drying on the ratified peace treaty—the Americans lost no time in launching their own ship to Canton for trade directly with the Chinese.

The harbor at Canton had been a distant dream to the seamen aboard the *Empress*. The city represented the gateway to China and its treasures: the entry to a world of mystery and magic, a place where fortunes could be made in trading for silk, tea, and porcelain. Canton had beckoned many adventuresome men before and would continue to attract others for years to come. No longer were Americans obliged to deal with the English in order to obtain the goods they desired.

The sailing of the *Empress* marked the beginning of American trade with China, a humming business that prospered until the 1860s. At the heart of this mercantile enterprise loomed the city of Canton, exasperatingly independent in its dealings with the West. They made strange bedfellows, the Chinese and the Westerners, so utterly intolerant of each other's ways. Insulated from the rest of the world, the Chinese were ignorant of the West and showed little interest in its culture. All foreigners—whether Asian, European, Arab, or American—were referred to as *i*, a word meaning, simply,

"non-Chinese." Moreover, the Chinese were not inclined to spread their culture by colonizing other lands. In spite of its vast coast, China saw no purpose in developing naval strength to protect it. Whoever chose to engage in trade with the Chinese was obliged to sail into Canton and follow the regulations—no matter how demeaning—as set forth by its inhabitants. It was worth the effort.

European trade with China
The rich potential of trade with China was known since the times of the Roman Empire. With a network of caravans and seacraft largely controlled by merchants at Alexandria, trading of silk and spices between the East and Europe was well established as early as A.D. 250-300. After the collapse of Rome it was not until the mid-13th century that trade was revived, when the Mongol Khans ruled. (It was during this period that Marco Polo narrated his travels to China from 1271 to 1295.) The Venetians, having exclusive trading privileges with the Turks, monopolized the overland spice trade with the East until the mid-15th century.

European passion for exploration stimulated the discovery

Above: *China Coast Clipper Ship "Isaac Reed,"* ca 1878. Oil/canvas, 26″ x 35″. Merchants commissioned Chinese painters to render ship portraits as souvenirs. Opposite: *The Hongs of Canton*, ca 1810. Oil/canvas, 16″ x 23½″. Each hong had a front building and others behind, connected by courtyards. Both courtesy Berry-Hill Galleries, Inc., New York.

of the East by means of sea navigation. Christopher Columbus was hunting for the lands of Cathay and Cipango (China and Japan) when he happened to stumble upon the New World. The Portuguese had located the passage around the Cape of Good Hope and by 1557 they had settled a small but permanent base in Macao, 80 miles south of Canton, from which they were permitted to visit the port city to trade at half-yearly sales in June and January. Portugal maintained a virtual monopoly on trade with China until the 17th century, when her supremacy was challenged by the Spanish, English, and Dutch who had sought their own routes to the East.

Political upheavals in China—the overthrow of the Mings by the Manchus—discontinued official trading with Canton and it was not until the port was reopened in 1699 that the English turned their attention from India to China. It was here that the British East India Company ventured frequently: 790 voyages to Canton between 1708 and 1802, a record unchallenged until the Americans launched the *Empress* in that fateful year of 1784.

Enter the Americans
Although the Americans had conducted comparatively little foreign trade prior to the Revolution, they were already geared up for the day when their independence would enable them to venture to distant lands by sea. The quantities of timber available in the virgin forests had already stimulated a flourishing ship building industry and there was a hardy

group of New England cod fishermen prepared to tackle any arduous seafaring journey.

Unlike the European trading companies, the American enterprises were exclusively private. In contrast to the organized operations of the Dutch and English—with their strong governmental backing—the American merchants entered trade as individuals, at their own risk, and offered the Chinese the advantage of smaller and quicker ships with youthful crews that could deliver goods in less time and at lower costs than the bulky East Indiamen vessels.

American traders provided commodities highly desirable to the Chinese. The economic self-sufficiency of China had been a constant irritant to the Europeans. Quite content with their own goods, the Orientals tended to export products that were vital to their culture—tea, chinaware, and raw silk—producing these items with great ease. Since Canton was the only port of entry, Western items were unknown throughout the vast interior of China and there existed little appetite for the commodities Europeans had to offer. Until the early 19th century, most of English trade with China was conducted at a trade deficit. Opium was to alter that course. As the English began to transport increasing quantities of opium from India to Canton, the Chinese thirst for the drug grew. Much profit was to be made by all those engaged in the

opium trade. In spite of many attempts made by the Chinese officials to eliminate the importing of opium, the demand only intensified. Between 1818 and 1834, over 50 million dollars in silver was carried off in British ships from China. Before too long China would face the threat of bankruptcy.

In finding items for trade, the Americans used characteristic ingenuity. At the outset, they had only ginseng, an herb the Chinese favored for its medicinal properties. But then they developed intermediate markets, most specifically in the Pacific Northwest. The New Englanders would sail there for as long as a year, trading with the Indians (not all of whom, incidentally, were friendly). In exchange for blankets, shoes, nails, and beads, the Yankees received abundant supplies of furs, particularly sea otter and seal pelts. Then the vessel would proceed to Hawaii and trade for sandalwood. What the Yankees received in exchange in China might net a profit five times the value of the original cargo.

The ship building industry in American reached new levels of sophistication. The late 1840s to the 1860s marked the height of the swift clipper ship trade. During this period New York emerged as the leading commercial city, followed by Boston, Philadelphia, Baltimore, Salem, Providence, Newport, and New Bedford. Howland and Aspinall's famous clipper *Sea Witch* was the fastest ship on the seas for three years after her 1846 launching. (Canton–New York: 74 days!)

The Civil War interrupted foreign trade and the English resumed their supremacy of the seas. After the War, steam had replaced sail and the opening of the Suez Canal in 1869—by cutting off the voyage around Africa and opening a route

Above: Tea service, 1795-1810, porcelain. Naval subjects on porcelain were a favorite for the American market, and tableware items could be easily individualized with monograms painted in Canton. The Henry Francis du Pont Winterthur Museum.

Portrait of Chinese Mandarin. Oil/canvas, 76″ x 45″. Portraits of Chinese merchants were a popular export item. This exquisitely executed canvas displays Chinese fineries: porcelain snuff bottle (in left hand) and spittoon, embroidery, rugs, silks, furniture; all objects desired by European and American markets. Courtesy Berry-Hill Galleries, Inc.

Top: *Portrait of Houqua* by Lam Qua, a pupil of George Chinnery, ca 1835. Oil/canvas. The hong merchant, Houqua, was a favorite among Americans. Paintings in the Western style were inspired by the presence of George Chinnery, an English painter who resided near Canton for over 25 years. Courtesy Childs Gallery, Boston. Above: Goose tureen, ca 1760, 14″ x 14″. The Portuguese were the first to trade with China in the 16th century and imported some of the most unusual examples of porcelain. Courtesy Fred B. Nadler, New York.

by way of the Red Sea—altered the nature of all international trade. An era had ended.

Chinese dealings with foreign devils

In spite of the tidy profits Westerners could expect from trading with the Chinese, there were humiliations to endure. The Chinese officials opened only one city to foreigners: Canton. This walled city was set back a short distance from the northerly bank of the Pearl River in Southern China. The waterfront and the suburbs flanking the city were the only areas designated for commerce. A beachhead of buildings (hongs) lined the shores of Canton: offices, warehouses, and living quarters leased by individual western nations. The entire trade conducted with China took place within a restricted area of less than one-quarter square mile.

To the Chinese all foreigners trading in Canton were *Fan Kwaes* ("foreign devils") and needed close watching. To supervise the movements of these devils, a hong merchant was required, an officially authorized individual licensed by and responsible to the officials above him. The hong merchant was a member of the Guild of Merchants formed, not by coincidence, only five years after the creation of the English East India Company. This Cohong, as the guild came to be called, provided the system by which the Chinese could control their trade and keep a watchful eye on the foreign devils.

The foreigner could select a particular hong merchant but after this minimal freedom all others were denied. Foreigners were supposed to remain in Canton—confined to a small area and under constant surveillance—only while engaged in unloading, loading, and disposing of cargoes; then they were to retire to Macao—80 miles away—or to some other place outside the bounds of China proper. Foreigners were forbidden to carry firearms, learn Chinese, or bring their women into the city. (Likewise, the Chinese were forbidden to learn English. So-called "pidgin" or "business" English was used for trading.)

The foreign merchant was entirely in the hands of the hong merchant. He had to sell his imports at prices set by the merchant and could deal with no other Cantonese. He had to buy all his return cargo from the same merchant at a price set by the hong. The hong merchant leased the company their factory buildings, paid duties, and acted as intermediary on all matters between Chinese government and client.

Although the monopoly of the Cohong made it possible for a merchant to lead a prosperous life, he did not have an enviable job. He was responsible for the behavior (often unpredictable) of the foreigners and for their financial stability as well. The merchant class in China was without rank or power, its office appointed—at a price—by the Emperor. Only a sharp and lucky merchant could amass a fortune under the system. The famous merchant Houqua was such an exception, an outstanding member of this group until his death in 1843, and a favorite among the Americans. Nevertheless, all the Chinese merchants were scrupulously honest. Foreigners never had written contracts and reported no problems.

From midsummer to midwinter each year the foreigners anchored for trading. It was essential to reach Canton before the late fall in order to take advantage of the favorable winds

in the vicinity of the China Sea. Trade was completed by the end of the year to profit from the winter season winds on the return voyage. After the last ship had departed the flags were lowered from the hong buildings and the factories closed their doors for the season. Even most of those foreigners who resided in the Orient were forced to leave Canton, and they took up residence in nearby Macao.

The Cantonese waterfront was a unique sight. The hongs lined up along the shore, each of these factories flying the flag of the nation having leased its quarters. On the water idled junks, sampans, and flower boats. The sight of this mercantile outpost left a vivid impression on any who beheld it, a vision frequently recreated in paintings.

In 1834 the charter of the British East India Company expired and British Parliament refused to renew it until the Cohong system was revamped. The Cohong was a daily reminder of the superior feelings entertained by the Chinese officials. The constrictions and indignities borne by the traders had become unacceptable. Likewise, the Chinese officials were increasingly alarmed at the disastrous effects created by the British imports of opium into China. Tensions from both sides exploded into the Opium Wars of 1842-44, regarded by the Chinese as a war over opium and by the British as a war to secure recognition of equality from the Chinese. The British victory over the Chinese resulted in the Treaty of Nanking—which opened the four additional "Treaty Ports" of Amoy, Foochow, Ningpo, and Shanghai—and the British takeover of Hong Kong. The opening of the Treaty Ports eliminated the oligopoly of the hong merchants and created a system of free enterprise within China through a new kind of merchant called a comprador (*mai-pan*), who functioned as a middle-

Top: *Canton: The Feast of Lanterns*, by W. Johnson, 1837. Oil/canvas, 21″ x 28″. Each year Americans in Canton could witness the famous Moon Festival, the lanterns ablaze in the harbor. Above: *The Hongs of Canton*, ca 1847, 18″ x 23″. Canton paintings are easily dated by knowing when certain structures were added or removed. We know this was painted shortly after 1847 because of the English church constructed after the Opium Wars. Both courtesy Berry-Hill Galleries, Inc.

man between China and the West. This shrewd, talented, and not-always-honest entrepreneur inevitably altered the complexion of Chinese trade for many years to come.

The trade in porcelain

Through the peak years of trading with China, the most lucrative commodities were tea and silks. Next in importance was porcelain. Reasonably profitable, porcelain's chief virtue was the role it played as ballast to the top-heavy sailing vessels. A chest of porcelain weighed 500 pounds, the equivalent of a chest of bricks, and could be placed easily in the hold of the ship to steady the vessel on its return voyage, and to protect the more fragile cargo.

The desire for porcelain in the West was spurred by the practical demand for tableware. The introduction of tea, and secondarily coffee and hot chocolate, created a demand for sturdy pots which would not be damaged by heat nor destroy the flavor of the hot beverage. Porcelain was the mystery material that Europeans had tried frantically to duplicate, with little success, until a comparable substance was developed in Meissen in 1708. Even with direct access to porcelain, however, European potteries could not compete with the low cost of Chinese export wares for several years to come.

Top: Blue and white oval hot water dish, 1770-1780. Porcelain, 15¼" long. The so-called "blue willow pattern," a popular mass produced item for export, illustrated the story of two lovers running off together. The traditional willow, figures, bridge, and boats are seen in the pattern. Courtesy Sotheby Parke Bernet, Inc., New York. Above: Detail of deep dish, 1770–1785, porcelain. The stages of producing porcelain at Ching-te Chen are depicted here. Winterthur Museum.

Blue Fitzhugh oval hot water dish and cover, early 19th century, 14⅜″ long. Immensely favored by English and Americans, the Fitzhugh pattern is characterized by floral clusters around the rim. Note pine cone finial. Courtesy Sotheby Parke Bernet, Inc.

The word porcelain derives from the China trade with the first Portuguese merchants in the 16th century who used sea shells as currency, calling them *porzella* ("little pigs") because of their clear pink color. When the Portuguese first saw porcelain it reminded them of the translucent shells and was given the appropriate name.

What we refer to as China trade porcelain encompasses all those pieces made in China more or less according to Western specifications and Western use. These primarily represented tableware objects. Decorative pieces, such as vases, were less common and figure groups quite rare. China trade porcelain varied in kind and quality and can be divided into two categories: first, inexpensive household wares, often made in plain white or blue and white; second, special order items—finer wares, including armorial china and other porcelains with decorations painted over the glaze and based on Western design sources. In the second category are found the most novel and colorful of the export porcelains.

The ingredients contained in porcelain include petuntse, which is formed by crushing a granite rock until—with the addition of water—the mass attains the consistency of clay. The petuntse is joined with a natural clay of fine texture and remarkably white color, kaolin. Geologically, this clay is close to petuntse, because it derives from the same rock, partially decomposed, from which petuntse is derived. When joined, the petuntse and kaolin reinforce each other. The quartz in the petuntse renders the material more fusible; the kaolin is sympathetic to modeling.

Even though unglazed porcelain is impervious to liquids after firing, the Chinese coated each item carefully with a feldspathic glaze to create a smooth, lustrous surface. The glaze is largely composed of petuntse, and because of its quartz content fuses completely to form the hard, glassy surface so characteristic of porcelain. Although *blanc de chine* wares were popular export items, most Chinese porcelains were embellished with colors applied under, over, or in the glaze. Because cobalt blue could be painted directly onto an unglazed body, the so-called blue-and-whites became a popular and inexpensive tableware for export.

The Chinese porcelains actually were created in the city of Ching-te Chen in Kiangsi Province some 600 miles from Canton. The location was ideal because of nearby resources needed for the manufacture of porcelain, and because of its easy access to northern and southern Chinese regions. The petuntse and kaolin were gathered in the mountains, carefully ground, washed, and refined into a creamy mixture, and shipped to Ching-te Chen in brick forms. The city of Ching-te Chen contained about 550 kilns and 3,000 to 4,000 factories. Fuel in the form of firewood and straw arrived in the city by river boat. (It required ten tons of fuel to maintain a single kiln at 1,500 degrees centigrade for 24 hours!)

In Ching-te Chen the most common sets of tableware were created for export. A visit to a contemporary pottery in China today will reveal that the methods of factory production have not changed since the time of the old China trade. An assembly-line system prevails: each person learns a single operation

Above: Dish and miniature tureen, ca 1876. Porcelain; tureen 2⅛″ high, dish 14½″ diameter. The amusing lettering on the plate and tureen indicates the signing of the American Declaration of Independence. Note that the facial features have been orientalized. Winterthur Museum. Below: Chinese export armorial circular tureen and cover, 1760. Porcelain, 10⅜″ wide. Forms are based on wooden models supplied by Western customers. Courtesy Sotheby Parke Bernet, Inc.

and performs it year in and year out. Some pieces are made on the wheel; others in molds. The rough shape may be thrown on the wheel, passed on to the next person for the addition of a foot, to a third person who places the cup in a mold attached to a wheel for a definitive form. The object is passed on from hand to hand in this way until it is complete. A single piece, it was reported by an eyewitness in the 18th century, could pass through the hands of 70 workmen before completion.

Unlike the porcelains made for the Chinese domestic market, those made for export to the West were shipped to Canton. Orders for the inexpensive household wares were filled in Canton and carried off in Western ships. Special orders were handled differently.

Prior to leaving the West, the chief cargo officer would accept special orders which he would execute as part of his trading. Since the ships were anchored in Canton for three months, there was generally sufficient time for the officer to place his order in the hands of the Cantonese merchant specifically authorized to handle these matters (a privileged group of shopmen permitted to deal directly with Western merchants, thereby bypassing the hong merchant). The order was sent to one of the local establishments where porcelains received final decoration. These establishments generally held a large inventory of undecorated pieces from Ching-te Chen so the order could be filled before the ship departed. (If new shapes or special underglazes were desired, models and patterns had to be sent to Ching-te Chen. In these cases a customer might not receive the goods until the next trading season, waiting two years for delivery of a special order.)

There were a number of establishments in and around Canton equipped to handle final decorations according to Western specifications. (Foshan, a few miles upstream from Canton, was an important center for this practice.) The craftsmen in these factories were trained to execute decorations from drawn images provided by the merchant. In imitating the drawings many mistakes could be made, of course, because of the workmen's ignorance of the English language. Examples of armorial porcelain reveal amusing mis-translations.

The system of decoration was the same as that of manufacture. Labor was divided according to specific tasks, passing from hand to hand, from one craftsman to the next, until the order was complete. The Chinese themselves did not place much esteem in Cantonese craftsmanship. Northern examples created for the Chinese domestic market were far more subtle in color and line than those created for export.

Europe had been trading in porcelain for almost a century before the Americans first arrived in Canton. China trade porcelain made for the Americans after that date was on a par with that produced for Europe. It differs from the European variety most specifically in the painted decorations, although there are frequently close resemblances. Among pictorial decoration, marine subjects were always an American favorite. American armorial decoration generally appeared in a patriotic context, substituting for the European preference for family armorials. Americans expressed the patriotism felt for their new republic: the death of Washington, the signing of the Declaration of Independence, and the ever-present eagle were favorite subjects of depiction.

Today's Canton

No longer need a foreigner fear the indignities experienced by the 18th-century traders. Now that the gates to Canton have been reopened at last, a welcome greeting awaits the visitor. The Canton of today still bears the mark of the international trade. The hongs are long since gone, but the European influence is evident everywhere in the city, particularly on the island of Sha Mian, where there are wide thoroughfares overhung with trees and lined with French-styled stone homes and apartments. Canton is still the trading city, and

Foshan pottery, 1979. Taken recently at a major pottery near Canton, these photos indicate that the factory tradition continues today: each stage of the operation performed by a different craftsman. Items are still created according to how Chinese interpret Western taste. A special order armadillo is being made for a Texan. Photos Susan E. Meyer.

conducts the major portion of its business twice yearly as it did in the 16th century with the Portuguese. In the spring and fall each year the Export Commodities Fair is open to foreign business and during these two months it is estimated that 25 percent of China's total foreign trade is transacted. Canton still represents the gateway to China. ■

Staffordshire

Transfer-printed tablewares, decorated with historic and scenic designs of interest to the American market, were produced in hundreds of Staffordshire potteries throughout the 19th century.

BY HELEN HARRIS

Blue Staffordshire, with its undeniable charm, illustrated one of the greatest romances on earth: the building of a new, great nation from a virgin land. Reflecting the pleasure and excitement of each successive step from the erection of fine new churches, customhouses, and hospitals to the completion of that awesome engineering feat, the Erie Canal, much of the progress of this country was commemorated by the Staffordshire potters on plates, platters, mugs, jugs, and pitchers.

The Staffordshire earthenware factories—over 200 of them, some well known but most obscure—became a special phenomenon in the potting world. When a world was being carved from a wilderness and a new nationality was arising from the flames of the Revolutionary War, mementos with a pictorial record of historical sites and structures seemed especially right and desirable. And as it happens, some of them have proved to be the only known records of our early buildings and historical sites since documentation—the original drawings and engravings from which they were copied—is now missing.

British wares found a ready market in the Colonies well before the Revolutionary War. Many people were willing to replace their woodenware and pewter with pottery made in Great Britain. (Only the most affluent could afford porcelain.) The first Josiah Wedgwood, who spearheaded the practice of shipping quantities of tableware to America, felt that most Colonists could not afford elegant and expensive china, and he was right. The company confined its exports to the simplest ceramic wares—even seconds. Feeding this market was possible for Wedgwood and other Staffordshire potters because of mechanical progress that allowed for quantity manufacture. (This early earthenware earned heavy usage; undoubtedly few pieces have come down to us.)

Although Wedgwood was the first to see the advantage of an American market, the firm under his grandson Josiah III probably did not produce any of the blue-and-white ware so popular in this country during the first half of the 19th century. Later, from 1880 to 1900 and then again in 1931, Wedgwood made attractive plates of this type to the specific order of the Boston firm Jones, McDuffie & Stratton. William Plummer & Co. of New York also distributed the wares.

British potters suffered, and a number went out of business, when trade was restricted during the British-American conflicts. A lucrative trade before and after the Revolutionary War was suspended again after the war, between 1808 and 1814. A United States embargo (first through the Embargo Act and then, in 1809, through the Non-Intercourse Act) forbade Americans to trade with France or England. All three countries experienced severe economic hardships during the Napoleonic wars and the War of 1812. The potters were anxious to resume trade with America, and to demonstrate their intentions they began to create many pro-American motifs. A famous Liverpool piece commemorated "The Long Embargo." Wedgwood and others in the industry had from the first been sympathetic to the American cause. Now wares were produced expressing sentiments that had the authorities chosen to pursue it, could have been considered treasonable. But freedom of expression appeared to be no problem as long as there was a good foreign market.

These patriotic pieces met with approval in America, where nationalistic feelings ran high. Many had known or seen the great patriots, and the new Republic was still a fresh reality. Washington had been dead for only 15 years, and Franklin an additional 9, when trade between Britain and

Above: Pitcher and wash bowl by Enoch Wood and Sons, ca 1826-1830. This vignette of Lafayette at the tomb of Franklin exemplifies the early 19th century fascination with memorial and tomb scenes. It is adapted from a drawing by D.W. Jackson. Right: The same pitcher seen in profile. It bears an impressed Enoch Wood and Sons mark. Both, Old Sturbridge Village.

America was resumed in 1814. Jefferson and John Adams were still alive watching the new nation grow. The patriots' portraits were used on pitchers, bas-relief plaques, and commemorative plates. These were not limited to the blue-and-white wares, nor were they the only subjects used to decorate blue Staffordshire.

Staffordshire pottery was made of a rather coarse clay, crudely potted. Imperfections on the pottery were cleverly hidden by deep blue transfer prints. This blue was one of the earliest colors. Americans particularly loved the rich tone of the strong cobalt, the most foolproof of the ceramic pigments. A light blue was more popular in England and on the Continent. Most transfer prints were made in deep blue between 1818 and 1830. Other colors, such as brown, green, purple, and pink, were introduced well into the 1840s. All enjoyed popularity until between 1850 and 1860, when few new American historical scenes were launched.

When potteries developed the transfer method of applying a pattern on a piece of pottery, they revolutionized the speed and cost of production. All ceramic designs had once been hand painted. With the transfer technique, a master engraving was used indefinitely. The pattern was engraved on a copper plate that was "inked," or filled with the enamel coloring mixed with a special printer's oil. The design was then transferred to a tissue paper treated with a preparation of soap and water. The paper was applied to the piece. After standing for a few hours, the paper could be softened in cold water and removed. Finally, after the piece had dried for several days, it was fired, and this burned out the oil. Subsequently it was dipped into a glaze and refired. This "underglaze" method of printing was most durable.

The ten-mile-long potting district of Staffordshire, known as "The Potteries," included Stoke-on-Trent (a city federated in 1910 that includes the old towns of Tunstall, Burslem, Hanley, Stoke-upon-Trent, Fenton, and Longton) and other communities of Smallthorne, Longport, Cobridge, Etruria, Barlaston, Land End, and Shelton. Blue-and-white wares were made by many Staffordshire companies, but the wares of only about 22 of them can be identified by their marks or recognizable motifs. In 1829 an estimated 50,000 people worked for the potteries in this district.

A distinctive border pattern is one of the most important characteristics of most plates and platters. Such borders are often adapted to pitchers, bowls, tureens, and their covers as well. While there are over 100 known borders, some 15 have been linked to specific factories. In two cases the factories remain to be identified.

In Staffordshire pottery, as in all ceramic wares, marks can be important. Unmarked pieces with a certain border design have been identified when the same border appeared on a marked piece. Manufacturers frequently changed their marks over the years, and these alterations often provide a clue in dating a piece. Books such as *Historical Staffordshire* by David and Linda Arman or *English China and Its Marks* by Thomas Ormsbee are excellent guides in this respect. However, the real sleuthing in the field of old blue Staffordshire can be undertaken from the face rather than the back of the piece, for much can be determined by studying the borders and the categories of subject and learning to recognize the work of the artist who designed the motif printed on the ware.

Reproductions of blue-and-white transfer-printed wares have been made by manufacturers over the years. The best way to recognize a 20th-century example is to examine the piece for wear and for weight. Many, but not all, old pieces show the signs of usage—hairline cracks or fine scratches in the glaze—and are often heavier than pieces made with later technical improvements. (Some, however, are in mint condition.) Also, with reproductions, there will be fewer or no printing irregularities on the pieces, more color uniformity, and less or no "flow"—the slight or pronounced blurring of the print often found on old pieces.

Life in the early days of this country, when big-city populations counted in the tens of thousands and communication and transportation were sparse and slow, may be seen in surprisingly vivid detail if one studies the many different Staffordshire scenes. However, the view of life then expressed by the artists in their engravings is a romanticized one. Every district had its important projects, and fine, new buildings were duly recorded. Blue Staffordshire provides a travelogue of 19th-century historic sites and of the growing nation. Government buildings, churches, libraries, banks, colleges, hospitals, and modes of transportation from sailing ships and early steamboats to railroads all appear. The founding fathers Washington, Franklin, Jefferson, and Adams, were commemorated, as was Lafayette's famous return visit and tour of every state in 1824. Vividly drawn scenes from battles and battle monuments and a handsome series of the arms of the 13 original states enlivened dinner parties and Thanksgiving feasts.

A valuable biographical list of artists from whose original paintings, drawings, and engravings the transfer designs were made was compiled by the late Ellouise Baker Larsen in her

Above, top: *Arms of Pennsylvania* platter, 21" long, made by Thomas Mayer, ca 1829. This platter is the largest of eight produced for Mayer's American series of *Arms of the States*. Twelve states in this series are represented on cups, plates, and various kinds of dishes, as well as platters. The seal of Pennsylvania seen here suggests the industries of that state, as symbolized by sheaves of wheat, a ship, and a plow. The New-York Historical Society. Center, above: 22½ platter by John Rogers and Son, ca 1816, depicts battle between the U.S. frigate Chesapeake and the British Shannon. Although this platter is medium blue, dark blue was generally preferred by American buyers. Europeans preferred light-blue tones, while still other colors—brown, green, purple and pink—became popular after 1845. The New-York Historical Society. Above: James and Ralph Clews platter, about 21¼ long, pictures Lafayette landing at Castle Garden, 1824. The Revolutionary War hero Lafayette was lionized upon his return to New York in 1824. The event was much commemorated on Staffordshire wares. The New-York Historical Society.

Even when pieces of historical blue Staffordshire are unmarked, they may be identified through a study of the distinctive border patterns which were signatures-in-design for the various major potteries of the Staffordshire district. Individual makers created special border designs—usually combinations of flower, leaf, fruit, and shell motifs—to accompany each specific series of historical views. These borders constitute a reliable gauge of authorship. Unless otherwise noted, all borders are dark blue.

Enoch Wood & Sons
shells, irregular center

Andrew Stevenson
flowers and scrolls

comprehensive book *American Historical Views on Staffordshire China.* Works by such famous painters as Benjamin West, Gilbert Stuart, Thomas Sully, Rembrandt Peale, Thomas Doughty, George Catlin, and Thomas Cole are reproduced on Staffordshire along with the designs of a host of skilled but lesser-known artists—Karl Bodmer, Thomas Birch, Abel Brown, Michele Corné, Alexander Davis, James Eights, Alvin Fisher, John Wesley Jarvis, and John Penniman, to name a few.

A number of the most significant potteries that produced blue wares are outlined briefly as follows:

Enoch Wood

Enoch Wood & Sons (1819–1846) is credited with some 80 historic scenes. The pottery was the most prolific source of

American views. It was located in Burslem, a town noted as an important pottery center as early as 1686. Enoch Wood, who has been dubbed the father of British pottery, was the youngest son of Ralph Wood, whose English earthenware figures and Toby jugs are well known. Ralph Wood's older son, Aaron, succeeded his father. Enoch, a successful sculptor, started a pottery business of his own in 1783 with his cousin, Ralph Wood, as his partner. James Caldwell joined the firm in 1790 and the pottery became known as Wood and Caldwell. Enoch Wood became sole owner of the pottery in 1819 and invited his sons into the firm. The pottery was called Enoch or E. Wood & Sons from 1819 until the Wood sons sold the pottery to misters Pinder, Bourne, and Hope in 1846.

Characteristic borders on Enoch Wood pieces include two versions of a seashell pattern, incorporating an assortment of

Drawings by Barbara Swing

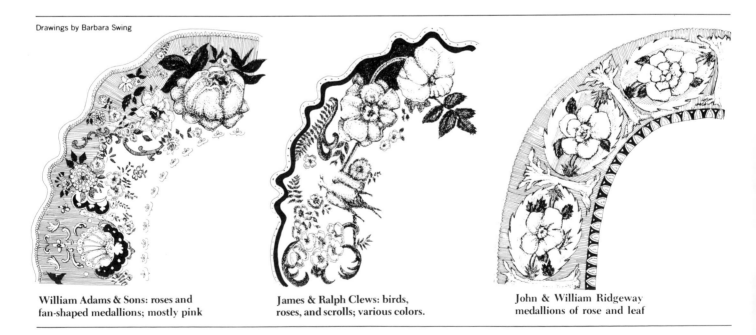

William Adams & Sons: roses and fan-shaped medallions; mostly pink

James & Ralph Clews: birds, roses, and scrolls; various colors.

John & William Ridgeway medallions of rose and leaf

Andrew Stevenson
mixed flowers

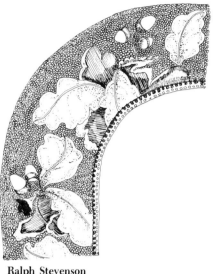

Ralph Stevenson
acorns and oak leaves

Ralph Stevenson & Williams
leaves and vines

shells from cockle to conch. The borders differ in the way they frame the plate's central scene. One irregularly frames the central design, the other surrounds the motif with a perfect circle. The latter most frequently decorated Enoch Wood plates. Wood also produced plates with borders of flowers and foliage and flowers and fruit. A scroll design broken at regular intervals by cartouches with miniature scenes or mottoes such as "America Independent July 4, 1776" was used on the *Landing of the Fathers* series, which portrayed the landing at Plymouth Rock.

The Wood pottery designed a number of kinds of dinnerware decorated with marine subjects, including several versions of *Cadmus*, the ship put at Lafayette's disposal during his visit in 1824, and of Commodore Macdonough's Victory. Other nautical designs showing ships were entitled *The Chief*

Justice Marshall, *The Constitution and the Guerrière*, and *The Chancellor Livingston*, an early steamboat.

A quaint view of the Baltimore and Ohio railroad with a cable train of coal cars on an incline at the mouth of a mine records the method by which coal was loaded in the early 19th century.

Views of the Catskills, the Tappan Zee from Greensburg, and other Hudson River views including the Highlands at West Point provide natural scenes of young America's terrain. The plates depict other views ranging from Niagara Falls and Table Rock at Niagara, to Passaic and Trenton Falls in New Jersey.

Wood's wares depicted public buildings such as the Capitol in Washington, the President's House—as the White House was then called, the Boston Statehouse, the Statehouse

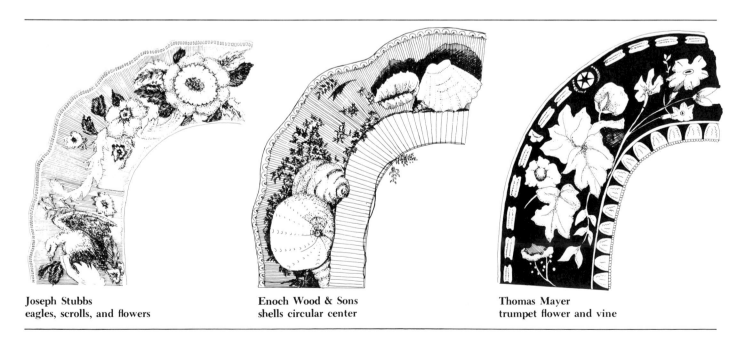

Joseph Stubbs
eagles, scrolls, and flowers

Enoch Wood & Sons
shells circular center

Thomas Mayer
trumpet flower and vine

in New Haven, and several views of Harvard College. The opening of the Erie Canal was commemorated by views of the entrance to the Hudson at Albany, the Aqueduct Bridges at Little Falls, and Rochester.

Andrew Stevenson

Andrew Stevenson was one of the first English potters to make blue transfer-printed historical American scenes. For years it was thought that Andrew Stevenson was a fictitious character and that the borders on Stevenson pottery were designed by a Ralph Stevenson. But studies have shown that Andrew did exist and managed a pottery from 1808 to 1829 in Cobridge. (He also was a coal merchant.) Andrew rather than Ralph has been credited with designing the borders.

Stevenson was the proprietor of a factory, W. Brownfield & Son, with a partner named Bucknall in 1808. Soon Stevenson operated alone. He made about 20 designs for the American market, and they were all good in workmanship and color. An Irish artist W. G. Wall, Esq., visited the States in 1818. While here, he made a series of sketches of notable American buildings, many of which were done for Stevenson. The pottery credited Wall on the back of the ware.

Characteristic Stevenson borders were flowers and scrolls and mixed flowers. The pottery's Lafayette series had three types of borders: raised or embossed floral motifs with applied enamel or luster; blue bands; and vine-leaf transfer prints. Andrew Stevenson borders also were taken from those of other potters, such as Enoch Wood's shell pattern.

Subjects for the center of plates, pitchers, platters, and such included a number of public buildings in New York—the Almshouse, St. Patrick's Cathedral on Mott Street (this church, which burned down, was a predecessor to the present structure on Fifth Avenue), City Hall, and Columbia College. There were also distant views of New York from Brooklyn Heights and Weehawk. Fort Gansevoort and Governors Island were also subjects, as were rural views of the Catskills on the Hudson River, the junction of the Sacandaga and Hudson Rivers, Troy from Mt. Ida, the view on the road to Lake George, Niagara (a sheep-shearing view), and Wadsworth Tower in Connecticut.

In 1819 Andrew Stevenson sold the works to Ralph and James Clews. Stevenson continued to produce wares with his mark until approximately 1829, but the factory with which he was involved has not been identified.

Clews

The Clews brothers, Ralph and James, manufactured earthenware from 1819 to 1836 in Cobridge. At first they made pale cream ware, but then they concentrated on blue transfer ware. Fifty-three American scenic or historical views made by the factory included such notable subjects as *The Landing of Lafayette at Castle Garden* and many Hudson River views—Baker's Falls, Fishkill, Fort Edward, Fort Miller, Fort Montgomery, (the town of) Hudson, Jessup's Landing, the junction of the Sacandaga and Hudson Rivers, Newburgh, and New York.

New York views depicted the City Hall, the Almshouse, the Insane Asylum, and Columbia College. Pittsburgh and

Philadelphia were also included with, for example, a view of the Fairmount Water Works on the Schuylkill in Philadelphia.

Among the Clews borders was a prominent design of birds, roses, and scroll and a unique *Chain of States* border with the names of 15 to 18 states shown on scallops of ribbon separated by stars. The already complicated border also incorporated flowers, fruit, and figures representing America and Independence as well as a medallion with Washington's portrait. The central views of wares with this border are necessarily small, comprising architectural subjects from private houses to public buildings. Only the White House has been identified among them.

James Clews went to America in 1836 and tried to set up a pottery in Troy, Indiana, but failed miserably. The clay was not right, for one thing. For another, there was a lack of competent help.

J. & W. Ridgway

J. & W. Ridgway was a pottery owned by brothers John and William. There are conflicting stories about the history of the Ridgway works. One says that the brothers' uncle George and father Job formed the Bell Bank Works at Hanley (they called it Shelton then) in 1792. Job retired from Bell Bank in 1813 to build Cauldon Place Works. The Ridgway brothers took over the Bell Bank Works when their uncle retired about 1824. Another version has it that Job started the business in 1802 and that his sons took over in 1814 at his death. According to this story the firm changed its name that year from Ridgway & Sons to John & William Ridgway. The brothers broke up their partnership in 1830. William kept charge of the Bell

Bank Works and John took over the Cauldon Place Works.

In any case the Ridgways produced the only American views made by the firm from the Cauldon Place Works. The series reflected the altruistic bent of their characters, for they were noted for their philanthropy and civic interests. Rather than scenery, the Beauties of America recorded important buildings—hospitals, colleges, churches, and other public institutions.

The hospitals included the Pennsylvania Hospital, Philadelphia; (Massachusetts General) Hospital, Boston; Insane Hospital, Boston; Deaf & Dumb Asylum, Hartford, Connecticut; and almshouses in Boston and New York.

Churches were represented by the Octagon Church and St. Paul's Church, Boston and Staughton's Church, Philadelphia. Two libraries in the series were Boston's Atheneum and Philadelphia's Library.

Public buildings included Baltimore and Charlestown money and stock exchanges, a Savannah bank, a Boston court house, a Philadelphia customs house, a Boston Statehouse, the Washington Capitol and New York City Hall.

The border of this series is unmistakable—roses and leaves conventionalized as medallions giving a chain effect.

John Ridgway

After his brother left, John Ridgway carried on the Cauldon Place Works in Hanley and produced work of high caliber until 1855, when he retired. He was made potter to the Queen in 1851.

The Cauldon Place Works is credited with a *Log Cabin* series in various colors including light blue, as well as a view of the Capitol in Washington in dark blue. Yale University in light blue is attributed to this factory.

William Ridgway

William Ridgway, once independent of the J. & W. Ridgway factory, operated Bell Bank Works in Hanley. Eventually he took his son, Edward, into the firm. William Ridgway was a dynamic businessman, acquiring other factories until six potteries fell under his management. William's American series included landscapes, some of which were in light blue.

A view of Albany, Caldwell on Lake George; Columbia Bridge on the Susquehanna, Crow's-Nest from Bull Hill (Hudson River), Harper's Ferry from the Potomac side; and the Narrows from Staten Island are among the 25 or so American scenes the pottery produced.

A *Catskill Moss* series of similar American subjects was printed in light blue. The distinctive border shows sprays of moss on a mosaic-like background.

Joseph Stubbs

Joseph Stubbs was a potter who established the Dale Hall (Dale Hole) Works at Burslem in 1790. He produced only a few designs for the American market, but they are considered to be of high caliber in every respect—design, color, and finish. The Boston Statehouse platter is one of the best known. Stubbs also designed a very busy plate with a view of a shore hotel at Nahant, Massachusetts.

Other scenes were laid in and near New York, including a view of Hoboken in New Jersey, the East River, New York Bay, Dr. Mason's Church, Park Theater, and two views of City Hall. There were two views also of Philadelphia: Woodlands and the Race Street Bridge and Upper Ferry Bridge over the Schuylkill River.

The important Stubbs border is striking, with spread eagles (four on the platters and three on the plates) intermingled with leafy scrolls and flowers. A fine crimped line encircles the central view. Another border features full-blown roses.

Thomas Mayer

The Mayer family—Thomas, John, and Joshua—bought the Dale Hall Works when Joseph Stubbs retired in 1829. Until recently it was thought that the firm stopped making wares for the American market except for the plates by Thomas Mayer showing the seals of the 13 original states. The border on this *Arms of the State* series contained trumpet flowers and vines with pinwheel motifs set at quarterly intervals in a husk band on the outer edge. There was also an inner border of pointed scallops. However, *Lafayette at the Tomb of Frank-*

lin and *Lafayette at the Tomb of Washington* are two subjects that have come to light on a sugar bowl and teapot, and are thought to be attributable to the Dale Hall pottery. But the American wares are marked "Stoke" and not "Burslem" and must refer to the Cliff Bank Works, a pottery Thomas Mayer also operated. Joshua, who was considered the most clever of the brothers, was said to have died of overwork.

Ralph Stevenson & Williams

Ralph Stevenson of Cobridge was known to have been working independently as a manufacturer in 1815 and produced a group of over 35 fine designs for the American market. On his wares the name Stevenson or the initials R.S., R.S.W., or R.S.&W. appeared. It is generally accepted that W stood for Williams, his New York agent. Evidently, sons of Stevenson joined him around 1834, for in that year the name became R. Stevenson & Sons. The pottery closed six years later.

Two borders were used that are easily identified. One consisted of oak leaves and acorns against a finely dotted background. The other was a wreath of vines and leaves.

Views of the buildings in Boston include the Hospital, Almshouse, Atheneum, and City Hall. In New York it was the Battery (Flagstaff Pavilion), the Esplanade and Castle Garden, City Hall, Almshouse, Hospital, Insane Asylum, Fulton Market, Columbia College, Fort Gansevoort, and St. Patrick's Cathedral on Mott Street. Philadelphia's Masonic Hall and Pennsylvania Hospital were shown, and in Washington the President's House and the Capitol. There are also less familiar subjects like Shipping Port of the Ohio, Kentucky, and Riceborough, Georgia.

Wares marked R.S.&W. feature views of Harvard and Columbia, the Philadelphia Water Works, the American Museum (Scudder's), and views of the Nahant Hotel near Boston.

William Adams

There are four known potters with the name William Adams. Three were cousins and the fourth a son of one of the others. Between them they owned potteries in Stoke, Tunstall, Burslem, Cobridge, and Greenfield. Larsen in *American Histor-*

ical Views on Staffordshire China carefully disentangles their histories and states that only one made American views.

Most notable is the view *Mitchell & Freeman's China and Glass Warehouse, Chatham Street, Boston*, which bore a foliage border with its identifying pine tree on one side.

Rogers

The Rogers brothers, John and George, built a Staffordshire pottery in 1780 that was later operated only by John when his brother died in 1815. He took his son, Spencer, into the firm, and the pottery continued until it was sold in 1842.

Five or six American designs were produced in dark blue, including three views of the Boston Statehouse. Its border of roses and forget-me-nots is easily identified.

Two marine subjects, entitled *The Chesapeake & Shannon* and *The Shannon Frigate*, were made in a medium blue with sprays of flowers, leaves, and mottled seashells in the border.

Other Staffordshire potters whose names have come down to us are E. J. Phillips & Co., J. & J. Jackson, Thomas Godwin, S. Tams & Co. (also Tams & Anderson and Tams, Anderson & Tams), Joseph Heath & Co., Charles Meigh, Thomas Green, Mellor Venables & Co., and J. B., F. M., and Thomas Ford. Few of these potters made wares in the popular deep blue but they all produced designs with American themes.

A collection of blue Staffordshire can be assembled from many points of view—by historic buildings, by regions, by personalities, or by specific artists' engravings such as those of W. G. Wall, which were used by four manufacturers. Of course there were many subjects other than American scenes produced and many colors other than blue (such as black, brown, maroon, purple, green, tan, yellow, and pink) imported to this country, but the deep or dark blue was always most plentiful. It is still fairly plentiful, and the scarce or rare items can be found often enough to make the search enticing. Many wares are still to be identified as to factory, and new and unrecorded scenes occasionally appear. A few scenes are known to exist but have not been seen even by experts. A historical journey into America's past by way of 19th-century blue Staffordshire promises adventure. ■

Occupational Shaving Mugs

Shaving mugs decorated with occupational motifs came into vogue shortly after the Civil War. They were left at the barber's between weekly visits so each customer could lather up from his individual container.

BY RICHARD F. SNOW

". . . ANYTHING IN ART OR NATURE, from a Cigar to an Ocean Steamer, or from a Mosquito to a Range of Mountains, done in the most artistic manner. . . ." With this energetic boast, the 1888 catalogue of the Smith Brothers Barber Supply Company in Boston introduced its line of decorated shaving mugs. The hyperbole was necessary; the Smith brothers were competing with dozens of barber-supply companies and china decorators, all turning out bright, intricately painted mugs for an immense market.

At the turn of the century, the barbershop was a great center of small-town life. There, on Sundays, the men would gather to gossip, exchange news, haggle, leaf through the virulent, pink pages of the *National Police Gazette*, and, of course, get shaved. The shaving soap was kept in mugs, and the regulars liked to have individualized ones. Some of these merely bore the owner's name, but the more prominent local artisans and farmers often reflected the pride in trade common to the era by paying a dollar or more to have a painting of their occupation put on the cup as well. The mugs were kept in oak racks, and when, say, the town carpenter entered the shop, the barber would reach for a mug that had his name on it in ornate gold lettering, above a carefully executed scene of a man sawing through a plank.

These occupational shaving mugs are a unique American phenomenon. They came into vogue shortly after the Civil War, but nobody knows just how the custom got started. A New Jersey mug collector, Warren Moore, believes it stemmed from European china decorators who emigrated to the United States; he supports his theory with an 1860s French barber bowl decorated with the name of the owner, a painting of a locomotive, and the word *chauffeur*. However the custom may have begun, it spread rapidly, and by the 1890s every barbershop in America had its rack of mugs.

Customers ordered the cups from their barbers, who in turn got them from barber-supply companies. They cost the barber up to $2.50 for particularly florid examples, and the customer whatever profit the barber could graft on to his price. The companies kept the barbers well-supplied with catalogues filled with handsome chromolithographs of decorated mugs and peppy sales copy: "These catch your eye"; "None handsomer than these." Occasionally the companies sent out large posters—now extremely scarce and valuable—showing their line.

Virtually all the mugs themselves came from the great European porcelain manufactories (the few made of American china tend to be squat and dingy), and after the McKinley Tariff of 1891 they had to have the country of origin stamped on the bottom—"T&V, Limoges, France"; "Leonard, Vienna, Austria." They were shipped by the gross, naked and virginal, to the American barber supply companies, there to await the attentions of the mug decorators.

The Koken Barber Supply Company of St. Louis was the largest of these companies, with as many as nine men working in its decorating department. They put in a long day—8:30 to 5:30, half an hour for lunch, six days a week—and each could finish about ten mugs daily. A decorator would select a mug

Opposite, upper left: Fireman's mug, ca. 1880. These mugs have always been popular with collectors. Few are for sale because they were among the first mugs to be collected—usually by people interested in fireman memorabilia. The painting on this early example has a flat, primitive quality. Opposite, upper right: Brickstriper's mug, ca. 1900. You can see the striper on a little scaffold near the top of the building. Opposite, lower left: Greenhouse owner's mug, ca. 1900. Highly detailed, this mug even shows the flowers in their pots. Opposite, lower right: Miller's mug, ca. 1880. This mug depicts the water wheel in operation and the miller with his bag of flour.

No. 1062.

No. 1078.

No. 1056.

No. 1070.

No. 1022.

No. 1044.

Ask us to quote you our special cash prices or inform you regarding our easy payment plan.

"Working steadily, an artist could finish around ten mugs a day."

and, steadying his arm on a small box on his worktable, paint on the desired occupational symbol. Occasionally he worked from a tissue-paper template with a design punched in it, which he held against the cup and dusted with charcoal, giving him a faint outline to follow. But there were no templates for the more unusual trades, and most work was done freehand. Decals were never used, and no two paintings were ever exactly alike.

After the initial brushwork, the mugs were fired—70 at a time at the Koken Company—in a coke-burning kiln. Often, the decorator added more colors and fired the mug again. Then he would put on the gold name and, using a turntable, brush on delicate gold bands. It was real gold. Edgar Wendell, a veteran Koken employee whom Robert Blake Powell tracked down while working on his privately published book *Antique Shaving Mugs of the United States,* remembered that his boss would "save all the rags . . . used to clean the brushes . . . till the end of the year, when we would burn them to retrieve the gold nugget—which we sold and split among us. About $20 in all."

Finally, the mug went again to the kiln and then, with the gold polished, was shipped off to proclaim to all who entered the barbershop that its owner was a fireman—or a tinsmith, or a miller, or a bartender—and proud of it.

The quality of the painting varied greatly from mug to mug, according to the skill of the decorator. At their worst, the scenes are crude but engaging; at their best, they are superb examples of American folk art. Though mugs frequently carried the mark of the supply company that sold them, they were rarely signed by the artists themselves, and little is known of the men who did the painting. (With few exceptions, decorators were men). Among those whose names have survived are Curt Grimm, for years foreman of the Koken decorating department; A. Riedel, a New York City china decorator who liked to work in muted colors; Philip Eisemann of Lancaster, Pennsylvania, who did large, clean, simple paintings; and the ill-starred J. R. Voldan, who returned to his native Czechoslovakia and disappeared during World War II. But many artists of equal skill simply never took the trouble to put their names to their work, and a signature has little effect on a mug's cost.

The value of a mug in today's market depends not only on the quality of the painting, but also on the rarity of the occupation represented. A well-painted carpenter is not nearly as valuable as a sloppily-done steeplejack. It seems as if every butcher in the land had to have his own mug, and they are the ones most commonly found today. A good example would not bring much more than $65. A bartender might cost $150, and a particularly fine livery stable or horsecar could fetch twice that. But an undertaker, by far the scarcest of the common occupations, is worth a lot more; one is reported to have gone

Above: Steam-powered tractor engineer's mug, ca. 1890. The illustration has an almost photographic realism. Below: Railroad engineer's mug, ca. 1890. A great many old mugs relating to the railroad survive today. Opposite: Page from *Kraut & Dohnal Barbers' Supplies,* a catalogue for barbers, ca. 1905. These catalogues, issued by supply companies, offered everything the barber could possibly need—including mugs. Studio 9, author's collection.

"The value of a mug depends on the rarity of the occupation represented."

at auction in California recently for $800. Mugs—and the barbershop "club" tradition—were a working-class phenomenon, and designs representing professionals—doctors, lawyers, architects—are rare and costly. One-of-a-kind mugs such as a bee keeper or a tightrope walker are worth whatever the most ardent collector can be persuaded to pay for them. The value of any mug is reduced as much as two-thirds if the gold lettering of the name is rubbed away, and the beginning collector must beware of simple decorated mugs which occasionally are offered as occupational; one design, for instance, which has the owner's name surrounded by dark purple drapes, is frequently sold as either an actor's or an undertaker's mug.

Though of slight value, such nonoccupational mugs are, at least, authentic. Fake occupationals, however, have been around for years; the pioneer collector W. Porter Ware was complaining about them as early as the 1940s. Most are fairly obvious—clumsy lettering is about the surest giveaway—but some are very well done indeed. As with any other antique, the best way to be able to spot fakes is to study the real objects. (Only a few museums around the country, such as the New-York Historical Society in New York City and the Atwater Kent Museum in Philadelphia, have exhibits.) The most common reproductions were not intended to fool anybody, though they quite often are offered as originals. Usually marked "Sportsman" on the bottom, they were issued as novelties by the Warner-Lambert Pharmaceutical Company during the early 1950s and can be spotted easily because, instead of the owner's name, the gold lettering identifies his occupation: "The Doctor," "The Engineer," "The Fireman."

Colorful though they are, these Sportsman mugs are poor seconds to the strong colors and bold, ingenuous designs of the originals. The decorating companies continued to produce them into the 20th century, but when, in 1903, King C. Gillette patented his safety razor, the shaving mug was doomed. As men began to shave themselves, enforced Sunday closings further cut into barbershop business. Finally, World War I taught a generation of young men to do their own shaving. By 1920, Curt Grimm, who once had eight men working by his side at Koken, was the company's sole remaining mug decorator. Koken shut down the department in 1923. A few china-decorating companies hung on until the thirties, but the custom had died.

In the 1940s, George Neeley, who had put in half a century behind a barber chair in Kansas City, said, "In the heyday of the old Westport [Road] I had almost 200. . . . mugs in my shop. . . . All types of men had the mugs, business men, working men and farmers. I had customers as far as 40 miles away who got in once a week to use their mugs. . . .

"I don't believe," he added gloomily, "men ever will go back to the custom." ∎

Opposite, top: Butcher's mug, ca. 1870s. Although the butcher's mug is common in its ordinary version, which shows the head of an animal, this mug is highly prized because it depicts the inside of the butcher's shop with great detail. The value of a mug depends on two things: the quality of the painting and the rarity of the occupation represented. However, a well-painted carpenter is not nearly as valuable as a sloppily done steeplejack. For an extra dollar, telegraph operators, railroad workers, steam-shovel operators, bank tellers, photographers, bakers, carpenters and others could all have personalized mugs made. Opposite below: Boilermaker's mug, ca. 1900. The tools of the boilermaker are depicted on this carefully detailed mug. Left: Barber's mug rack, ca. 1900. Customers ordered their personalized mugs from their local barber, who paid as much as $2.50 for the particularly florid examples. After the freshly painted mugs arrived, the barber stored them in an oak rack like the one pictured here, which was known as a 20-hole rack. After World War I forced a generation of young men to shave themselves with Gillette's new safety razor, the personalized shaving mug was doomed. By 1925, most of the decorating companies had closed. Studio 9, author's collection.

Historical Flasks

Colorful glass flasks, impressed with historic and commemorative designs, were blown in full-sized molds to satisfy the demands of thirsty and patriotic Americans.

BY JOHN P. GUTTENBERG, JR.

The consumption of liquid spirits has been part of our culture from the beginning. But only in the 1800s—from about 1815 until 1875—did the container have an importance equal to that of its contents. The development, sale, and use of the glass flask made drinking somehow more accessible. In the process it also stimulated a burgeoning domestic glass industry, gave vent to an early form of advertising, became a force in political campaigns, and contributed a remarkable folk art form to our native craftsmanship.

There is no other category of American glass so rich and varied in its subjects, forms, and colors. It has been said that American history can just about be traced through the subjects used on glass bottles, especially flasks, so varied are the designs. There are flasks in all shapes and sizes: squares, ovals, log cabins, fiddles, cornucopias and calabashes in colors of rose, blue amethyst, aquamarine, purple, amber, pale and dark green, and yellow.

The historical flask may not rank with the ax, the hoe, or the flintlock in building a young nation, but surely it was a familiar companion to those who labored at the forge or in the forest or field. And while it did not enhance literacy, elevate morality, or promote reasoned debate, it eloquently bespoke the venerated symbols of a proud, young republic.

Unique among American-made objects of artistic or antique value, the historical flask chronicles and reflects our nation's social, economic, and political history from the War of 1812, through the opening of the frontier, and into the Industrial Revolution.

Glassmaking in colonial days

Glassmaking was among the first industries in the earliest colonial settlements. A glassworks was constructed at Jamestown, Virginia, in 1609 for the purpose of making glass beads and bottles for trade with the Indians. But it was not until the middle and the late 18th century that glassmakers in the Colonies added a more decorative aspect to practical objects. The manufacturers Caspar Wistar in South Jersey, Henry William Stiegel at Manheim, Pennsylvania, and John Frederick Amelung of Frederick County, Maryland, were notable for the earliest domestic refinements in both the glassblowing process and its products.

Caspar Wistar established the first successful glass manufactory in 1739. For the most part, the glassware produced in his works was free blown—formed by manipulating a bubble of molten glass at the end of a blow pipe at just the right temperature. Blown glass can be ornamented in several ways: by crimping or making flutes and dents, by trailing or applying glass in a thread or ribbon to the surface of the piece, and by prunts or seals which are applied as hot gathers of glass and then tooled into motifs. The Wistar shop is especially known by collectors for the after-hours pieces made by its glassblowers for family and friends.

In 1763 H.W. Stiegel built his first glasshouse and by 1769 he had established two more. Following the English and German tradition Stiegel's glassware was decorated with engraving, enameling or pattern-molding. In pattern-molding, the glassblower would blow the gather of molten glass into a metal cup-like mold (usually set into the floor of the factory), carved with a pattern inside. Once the parison—or bubble of glass—was impressed with the pattern it was withdrawn from the mold and the glass was blown further, causing the pattern to expand until the item reached the desired shape and size. Glass created this way is often referred to as Stiegel-type.

Clockwise from bottom: Most American mass-produced flasks, including the Washington-Jackson commemorative flask here, ca 1828-50, were blown into hinged, full-sized molds. The Corning Museum of Glass. So-called "Pitkin" flasks, like the next one, were made by the German half-post method, requiring a double gather of glass. The New-York Historical Society. Yellow green sunburst flask, 1815-30. Courtesy Robert W. Skinner, Inc. New England Masonic flask, ca 1818-25, and the railroad flask. The Corning Museum of Glass.

John Frederick Amelung was the next glassmaker of note. His shop, the New Bremen Glass Manufactory, operated from 1784 to 1796. A German by birth, Amelung imported highly skilled German craftsmen, several of whom engraved and inscribed presentation pieces. The quality of engraving that decorated many of these pieces was considered equal to that done in Europe.

It is speculated that Amelung's works in Maryland created the prototype for the 19th-century flask. According to William C. Ketchum, Jr., one of the resident glassblowers blew a clear pint flask engraved with the name of Francis Stenger, a glassmaker at an early New Jersey factory. This presentation piece is dated 1792 and may be regarded as one of the first examples of glass made to commemorate a trade, since the symbol of a bottle—trademark of the glassworks—appears on one side along with a Masonic symbol signifying Stenger's membership in that group. In its flat, semi-ovoid shape and plain lip this vessel is quite similar to later flasks, particularly those made in the period from 1800 to 1825.

But it was in the first two decades of the 19th century that the historical flask as we know it was born. During that period several factors combined to affect both the form of the flask and the burgeoning industry which produced it.

Blown-mold technique

In about 1815 a more efficient technique came into use; it involved blowing the molten glass into fullsize molds that were hinged in several parts. These hinged molds contained a patterned decoration and were in the shape of the final object, thus, the descriptive term "full-size molds." This technique, which actually dated back to the Roman Empire, was especially suited to mass production of decorative bottles for rum, gin, and whiskey.

Resurrecting this technique in the early 19th century was a boon to the brisk commercial trade in bottled spirits that was found in the English and European markets and that was spreading at home as well. The early migrations into the frontier west of the Alleghenies established whiskey as a prized commodity for barter, not to mention its value in helping sustain life in a pioneer wilderness.

The years immediately following the War of 1812 were beset by a sagging economy and a downturn in the national spirit. Glassmaking was clearly an industry that could help boost the economy. The design and production of decorated whiskey containers also was seen as a vehicle for reaping profit from a deeper thirst for national identity and patriotic inspiration.

Figured flasks

The Pitkin Glass Works of East Manchester, Connecticut, which operated from 1783 to 1830, probably produced the first quantities of commercially available flasks; Pitkin was the first glassmaker to actually advertise his flasks. In 1817 he advertised an offering of 200 "figured" pocket bottles. Until this date Pitkin's excursions into flask making had been restricted to pocket bottles in the German half-post method with fine ribbed designs in a swirl pattern. (The halfpost method involved two gathers of glass. The first gather or post

The early amethyst Stiegel-type flask, this page, was blown in a one-piece ribbed pattern mold, removed, and pinched with a tool to form the characteristic diamond pattern. Metropolitan Museum of Art, gift F.W. Hunter, 1913. Inset: rare blown amber glass flask attributed to the Ellenville Glass Works. Courtesy Sotheby Parke Bernet, Inc. Flasks on opposite page are all of the two-mold blown type made after 1815.

Flags, soldiers, cannons, anchors, and stars frequently appear on patriotic flasks, but the eagle was perhaps the most popular symbol. Eagle flask, above, of blown-molded green bottle glass, bears profile of Columbia on reverse. Ca 1820–1840. Corning Museum of Glass. Right: A variety of full-mold blown "scroll flasks" in shades of aqua, deep blue-green, olive, and cobalt were made ca 1845–1860. Courtesy Robert W. Skinner, Inc.

was redipped and covered with a second gather, called the half post since it did not extend entirely over the first gather.)

The key departure was the use of the term *figured*, taken to mean that the flask body had been decorated with a figural design molded in low relief. Similar bottles were apparently in production by other New England glass houses—such as those at Keene, New Hampshire, and Coventry, Connecticut—around the same period or soon thereafter. These early examples were adorned on both sides with heavy-ribbed sunburst designs. Figured flasks have been divided into two classes: historical and decorative. The latter, to which the sunburst belongs, comprises the smaller number of designs.

It is worth noting that experts and collectors alike have applied a number of terms to figured flasks, making liberal use of the words *commemorative, pictorial, decorative,* and *historical*. Only the latter is generally accepted to include all of them. Perhaps that is because all flasks were presumed to have either a familiar decoration or specific depiction that can be identified with symbols, people, or events that were characteristically American.

It is important to note as well that both the terminology and charting of known flasks has been a function of 20th-century collecting and scholarship. Edwin AtLee Barber first called attention to these bottles in his book *American Glassware*, published in 1900. He counted 86 varieties of flasks. Stephen Van Rensselaer, one of the great early collectors,

made an attempt to identify and categorize known flasks in his 1926 study, *Early American Bottles and Flasks*. George and Helen McKearin, father and daughter, presented the most detailed accounting of flasks in *American Glass*, written in 1941. The McKearins charted 396 separate and distinct flasks made from 396 different molds.

After years of work, Helen McKearin and Kenneth M. Wilson documented over 760 flasks in their 1978 tour de force *American Bottles & Flasks and Their Ancestry*. Over the past 50 years this record has been aided by the works of Harry Hall White and Rhea Mansfield Knittle—both of whom tracked the elusive Midwestern (Ohio, West Virginia, and Kentucky) cousins to the flasks of New England and the Middle Atlantic states.

And it was a collector, Edwin Lefevre, who, more than any other, first popularized the stories behind the historical flask in his *Saturday Evening Post* article on October 19, 1929. Lefevre resurrected dozens of historical milestones and meanings captured in glass flasks.

The majority of historical flasks fall into principal groupings. These include portraits of Presidents, presidential candidates, U.S. or foreign celebrities, flags, emblems, symbols, and insignia of societies.

George Washington dominates among Presidents. His bust appears on dozens of different flasks, many bearing the inscription "Father of His Country." Andrew Jackson and

Left, clockwise from the bottom: amber eagle flask by the New London Glass Works, 1860-1866; Lafayette-Masonic example by the Coventry Glass Works, 1824-1825; olive-amber Lafayette-Liberty Cup flask by the same company, 1824-1825; hourglass Masonic, Coventry Glass Works, 1813-1830, and a half pint eagle-cornucopia, probably Pitkin Glass Works, ca 1815-1830. All courtesy Robert W. Skinner, Inc. Dark olive medallion flask, possibly by Pitkin, ca 1820-30.

Zachary Taylor run a close second to Washington.

Jackson flasks were among the most popular during their day—and were probably the most political of all. Jackson, the first populist candidate from the new frontier, lost a bitter campaign to the patrician John Quincy Adams in 1824. Both men appeared on flasks in their second contest in 1828. It is said that pints of hard liquor bearing Jackson's likeness reached every corner of the frontier. One did not have to be able to read in order to recognize the hero of New Orleans in his tunic. Adams, on the other hand, was portrayed in less flattering terms—his hooked nose, set jaw, and receding hairline all drawn to accentuate his Brahmin credentials. In all probability this caricature was arranged by those who favored the election of our first populist frontier President.

With the campaign of 1828 the historical flask hit its stride as a political tool—a form of political "button" that was sought, sported, and saved. Since it also could be handed out easily (a pint at the time cost but a few pennies) and sipped pleasurably, we may assume that it influenced more than a few votes.

Campaign flasks inscribed for William Henry Harrison ("Hard Cider and Log Cabin") and John Tyler ("Old Tippecanoe") helped elevate electoral passions in one of the most turbulent election periods of our history. And in 1848 Zachary Taylor's successful campaign played to his role as a war hero. Flasks inscribed "General Taylor Never Surrenders"

abounded. Taylor's bust was often coupled with that of Jackson on the reverse side. It was a common practice to link a candidate to a former President or hero. Hence the appearance of Major Ringgold, a hero of the Mexican War, on a Taylor flask. The inscription "A Little More Grape Captain Bragg" also adorned one type of Taylor flask. This command, attributed to Taylor at the Battle of Buena Vista, assured the obscure Bragg no less a mention in history than the redoubtable Ringgold.

Perhaps the most interesting flask bearing presidential likenesses is the one paying tribute to both Thomas Jefferson and John Adams. These two giants among the Founding Fathers were not only lifelong political adversaries but also at times bitter enemies. Ironically both men died within hours of each other on July 4, 1826—the 50th birthdate of the nation they helped launch. It is no surprise that the only vessel created in tribute to these men is referred to as "The Firecracker Flask."

Other flasks of the mid-19th century were dedicated to other well-known heroes. DeWitt Clinton, who gave us the Erie Canal and promoted the railroad, was one. The Canal was opened in time for Lafayette's triumphant return visit in 1824-25. Both men appeared on opposite sides of the same flask as well as enjoying exclusive portrayals of their own.

Lafayette was the first non-American to appear on a flask, but not the last. Lajos Kossuth, the Hungarian patriot whose exile to Turkey and visit to the United States in 1851 re-

kindled our passion for freedom fighters, appeared on several flasks. So, too, did Jenny Lind. Brought to America by the inestimable promoter P. T. Barnum, her tour was enormously profitable. "The Swedish Nightingale" graced numerous calabash-type flasks—a bulbous bottle with an elongated neck resembling a decanter.

Fanny Elsser, a European dancer who made her American debut in 1840, was the inspiration for a flask depicting a ballerina. Elsser, Lind, and the head of Columbia (referred to as "Miss Liberty" or "The Liberty Cap") are the only three females ever to appear on flasks.

Lord Byron and Sir Walter Scott also appeared, joined on a single flask: the former ostensibly because he was an ardent champion of freedom as well as a romantic poet; the latter because his works were widely read in America.

People of heroic proportions were favorite subjects for flasks but did not dominate them. Large groups of flasks were dedicated to the most familiar symbols of a robust young country. The American eagle was perhaps the most pervasive of these emblems. Flags, stars, anchors, cannons, and soldiers were all popular themes.

A land of plenty with a bountiful agriculture was reflected in flasks bearing cornucopia, floral urns, sheaves of wheat, and ears of corn. The latter, carrying the inscription "Corn for the World," was produced in Baltimore, then the port which shipped more corn to foreign markets than any other. It is no coincidence that this one flask has been found in places around the globe—a small legacy of the merchant sailors who stocked them for long voyages.

Word of new gold strikes in the West coincided with a period of economic depression in the late 1850s. Rumor for the most part, it nevertheless stimulated unemployed workmen and bankrupt businessmen to seek their fortunes westward. The ensuing market for prospecting paraphernalia and associated travel items gave the economy a slight boost and momentarily diverted the national psyche from its other pre-Civil War woes. The rallying point for most Easterners was the well-known Pike's Peak. Hence the advent of a large family of flasks featuring a fully equipped prospector and the slogan "For Pike's Peak."

Possibly one of the most interesting as well as esthetic groupings of historical flasks were the Masonics. Freemasonry flourished during the Revolution and into the 1930s. It was socially prominent and politically important in every state. New York and New England were its special strongholds, and those areas began turning out exquisite flasks before 1815.

These items were distinguished by their representations of the arches, tools, and other symbols most frequently identified with Masonic orders. The reverse side of the flask often displayed an eagle or occasionally a bust of Jackson or Lafayette—both famous Masonic members.

The last Masonic flasks were produced about 1830 due to sinister events that took place in Batavia, New York, in the late 1820s. A man named William Morgan was denied his 33rd Masonic degree and, in a fit of pique, revealed the secrets of Freemasonry to the editor of the local newspaper. When published, the news traveled across the nation, and a

Above: Log-cabin shaped "Booz" flask, 1840, Shelburne Museum. Opposite page: Concentric rings surround the eagle in this three-mold blown pint flask, 1815-1825, probably made by the New England Glass Company. Courtesy Robert Skinner, Inc. This flask sold on April 16, 1980, for $7,200.

wave of contempt against this exclusionary fraternity drove it underground until after the Civil War. Morgan's unspeakable deed caused Masonic flasks to become among the rarest and most treasured.

Flasks owe their survival largely to the fact that glass was precious through much of the 1800s, thereby often making the container more valuable than its content. Flasks were refilled again and again by their owners. Hard liquor replaced malt as the national drink during the 1830s, making the flask the perfect container. Flasks were also attractive display items. Their range of subjects matched virtually every patriotic interest. And they were trusted companions to be cared for and possibly handed down from one generation to another.

These vessels of our history came into vogue as collector's items in the 1920s. Lefevre probably described this phenomenon best in his *Saturday Evening Post* article:

> I am justified in insisting that what collectors of antiques really collect are stories of people and periods and customs . . . that is, the comedy and tragedy of life. An historic flask is an ultimate antique . . . a flask is, in the first place, actually historic, not only in what it may commemorate, but in itself. A flask bearing the profile of Jackson is not alone a portrait in relief, it is a whiskey flask of Jackson's era.

In that respect, the historical flask and 19th-century America grew up together. ■

Jacquard Coverlets

In 1820, Joseph Marie Jacquard invented a revolutionary loom attachment that made it possible to weave a complicated floral-patterned coverlet in a single day.

BY MADELINE ROGERS

To the people who made and used them, 19th-century Jacquard coverlets were simply bedcovers. But they have a different meaning today. Because 50 to 75 percent of them were "signed" by the weavers who made them, these coverlets have assumed a double value: individually, as attractive antiques with a known history, and, collectively, as a sort of diary-in-cloth that records the history of a giant family—the "family" of professional weavers that lived and worked in the mid-19th-century United States.

Coverlet weaving existed from our country's earliest days,

when housewives made geometric-patterned coverlets dyed with imported and native dyestuffs. Complex ornamental coverlets were practically unknown, for to weave pictorial textiles required sophisticated equipment, craftsmen, and the kind of time that didn't exist in a struggling young nation.

That situation changed radically in the 1820s, when the Jacquard attachment, invented by Frenchman Joseph Marie Jacquard, was introduced into this country.

Jacquard's device, which could be attached to existing drawlooms, simplified the weaving of pictorial textiles in one way but complicated it in others. The device replaced some of the manpower with a machine that created patterns at the "command" of a set of punched cards, much in the way a music roll gives instructions to a player piano. However, the pattern designs had to be drawn on squared paper, the Jacquard cards punched and laced, and the pattern set up in the loom's cording.

"Jacquard coverlet patterns run to folk-inspired floral, medallion, bird, and botanical motifs and to designs symbolizing current events."

Opposite page: Cotton and wool Jacquard coverlet with eagles and peacocks, 19th century. The coverlet's corners provided a space for recording the weaver's or owner's name. This example commemorates George Washington. The Brooklyn Museum, gift of Mrs. Erna Burrows.
Above: Detail of double-woven blue and white coverlet. Brooklyn Museum, gift of Miss Marguerite Taylor.

With a Jacquard attachment, a skilled weaver could make a coverlet in a day—a process that formerly took weeks.

Though it simplified complex ornamental textile weaving, a Jacquard-equipped loom could be set up and maintained only by a skilled operator. As it happened, European weavers, displaced by advancing mechanization in their homelands, began to find their way here. With the Jacquard mechanism at their disposal, they were ready to supply housewives with ornamental coverlets. And the 19th-century housewife, weary of her spinning and weaving chores and hungry for the novelty of manufactured goods, was ripe to create a demand.

Gradually, the simple geometrics of the home-woven coverlets were replaced in popularity by the fulsome swirls and complex borders of the Jacquards, an early instance of the still-thriving throwaway ethos: Exit the homemade coverlet to the barn or attic; enter the more prestigious Jacquard, now elevated to "best-use" status.

Jacquard coverlet patterns run to folk-inspired floral, medallion, bird, and botanical motifs and to designs symbolizing current events such as the Centennial. Their complexity held a mighty fascination for the people of the day, but many of today's textile experts are not that enchanted: Gail Andrews, assistant curator of decorative arts, the Birmingham (Alabama) Museum of Art, characterizes many of the designs as "repetitive," Philip Curtis, a curator at the Henry Francis du Pont Winterthur Museum, is "not terribly fond of coverlets," but adds that "in terms of research, it's very interesting to follow coverlet weavers."

Curtis is not alone in that sentiment. Whatever an individual's feelings about the aesthetics of coverlets, many agree that the most interesting feature of the genre is often the information woven into a coverlet—information that can elevate even an artistically dull coverlet into an important link in the chain of textile history.

For reasons of fashion and status, many of the early 19th-century women who preferred these professionally made coverlets to their homemade counterparts also wished to have their ownership recorded in some way. And the professional weaver, like a craftsman of today, wanted to identify his handiwork. It consequently became a frequent practice to weave descriptive information into the coverlets. Often it was the weaver's name or a decorative trademark, and the date; sometimes the customer's name and age or the town name or even an advertising slogan of some kind.

If this practice had been limited to a scattered handful of weavers, it would be a mere curiosity, but since at least half of all Jacquard coverlets were marked in some way, the phenomenon is significant.

For years, the importance of these identifying marks was recognized by researchers, but little was done in the way of

Above: Double-woven red and white Jacquard coverlet signed J. Van Ness and dated 1849. Patriotic motifs were popularly used on Jacquard coverlets of the 1820s, 30s, and 40s. This example features portrait heads of Miss Liberty flanked by laurel branches, and a richly scrolled border with shield-bodied eagles in the corners near the motto "E Pluribus Unum." J. Van Ness worked in Palmyra, New York. Collection of Mr. & Mrs. Foster McCarl, Jr. **Left:** Double-woven blue wool and natural cotton coverlet, unknown weaver, ca 1830–1840. Made without the aid of a Jacquard attachment, this coverlet of characteristically simple geometric design contrasts sharply with the flowing, elaborate patterns created by the Jacquard weavers. The Art Institute of Chicago, gift of Mrs. Richard Folsom.

compiling the information in any systematic way. The appearance in 1978 of *A Checklist of American Coverlet Weavers*, compiled by John W. Heisey, edited and expanded by Gail C. Andrews and Donald R. Walters (Williamsburg, Virginia; The Colonial Williamsburg Foundation, 1978), has changed that. The book, published for the Abby Aldrich Rockefeller Folk Art Center, is the first attempt to study coverlet weavers and weaving on a national scale.

Prior to the book's publication, information was available from organizations like the Colonial Coverlet Guild of America, which published a checklist of its own holdings, or in regional studies like Pauline Montgomery's *Indiana Coverlet Weavers and Their Coverlets* (Indianapolis: Hoosier Heritage Press, 1974). But these sources were relatively limited in scope. *A Checklist of American Coverlet Weavers* (hereafter referred to as the Checklist) incorporates materials from these sources and others, providing an unprecedented opportunity for the collector to discover a coverlet's pedigree by flipping open a single book.

Until the Checklist, an individual could research the origins of most coverlets—particularly if they bore the weaver's name—but the task could take months and even years of arduous searching through secondary and primary sources—for example, newspapers of the period. Nor was there any guarantee that this patience would be rewarded. The search might end in a blank wall or, if the collector relied solely on secondary sources, with misinformation and half truths.

Any study of coverlets begins with the coverlets themselves, which contain a wealth of both implicit and explicit information. Some of these explicit features are obvious even to an untrained eye. To understand implicit features, such as the weave structure, it is necessary to study other coverlets comparatively to learn to "read" one's own. The effort will pay off in a deeper appreciation of the coverlet's merits and its creator's ingenuity.

- **Motifs.** Designs of coverlets, like those of many quilts, traveled across state lines and even into Canada. In addition, weavers, according to the Checklist, ". . . could purchase ready-punched patterns or design cards. . . ." The book cites an advertisement by weaver Josiah Cass, which states that ". . . he was ready to weave coverlets of every description, having just received new designs from New York."

By itself, a motif can't be used to pinpoint a weaver's identity or a coverlet's origins, but certain patterns are associated with particular weavers and regions. For example, the distelfink, a bird motif, is mentioned by Pauline Montgomery, who says it was "[by] far the most popular border with German weavers and those from Pennsylvania and Ohio."

Harold B. and Dorothy K. Burnham caution against drawing conclusions based on motifs alone. In their book, *Keep Me Warm One Night* (Buffalo and Toronto: University of Toronto Press, 1972), they describe the work of weaver John Campbell, whose borders feature an eagle grasping a thunderbolt. The natural assumption would be that these coverlets are American. In fact, Campbell emigrated from New York State to Canada, where he set up shop. In the Burnhams' opinion, this pattern ". . . is undoubtedly based on one Campbell used in the United States, the cards for which he brought with him. . . ."

- **Weave structure.** According to the Checklist, Jacquard coverlets were woven one of two ways: double cloth, in which the two sides are actually two separate layers woven together at regular intervals, and a single-weave twill, sometimes called Beiderwand.° The Checklist states, "A few generalizations about regional weaving techniques and weave structures can be made. . . . For instance, coverlets made in New York, New Jersey, Indiana, and Illinois most often are double woven, while those from Pennsylvania and Maryland

---

° *Although the term* Beiderwand *is widely used in this context, it is technically incorrect, according to Rita Adrosko, textile curator, the Museum of History and Technology, Washington, D.C. Beiderwand, she says, correctly refers to a type of reversible German bed curtain and not to weave structure. Dorothy K. Burnham has analyzed the different Jacquard woven "single" weaves in a chapter in* Studies in Textile History, *edited by Veronica Gervers.*

Below: Single-weave Jacquard coverlet of natural and light blue cotton warp and blue wool weft, signed by J. Denholm of Pennsylvania and dated 1844. Symmetrical arrangements of tulips and birds were often used by weavers of German descent working in Pennsylvania and Maryland. So-called "Beiderwand" (or single-woven) coverlets like this one were also made primarily in areas of German settlement. (The coverlets of New York, Indiana, New Jersey and Illinois tend to be double-woven. These areas were settled primarily by the British.) Art Institute of Chicago, gift of James Brown IV.

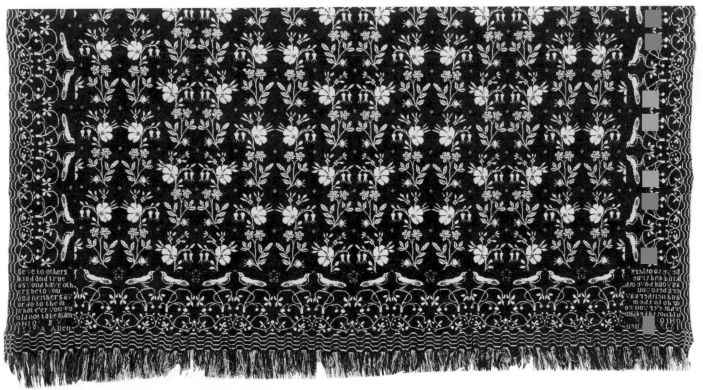

Above: Double-woven blue and white coverlet by A. Allen of Ohio, dated 1839. At least four coverlets by the weaver A. Allen of Highland County, Ohio, have come to light—an example identical to this one, but dated 1842, is held by the Newark Museum. The bird perched on a cherry branch, a border motif favored by A. Allen, has provided the basis for attribution to him of several unsigned quilts. Note the delicately stylized swamp-rose and rose hip motif of the central field. Left and below: A detail of the same quilt shows border inscription "Be ye to others kind and true as youd have others be to you and neither say or do to them whatever you would not take again." Both American Hurrah Antiques.

are generally single woven in the *Beiderwand* weave. The available data indicate that the majority of weavers who settled in the former group of states, especially New York and Indiana, came from the British Isles. Weavers in Pennsylvania and Maryland were usually German or of German heritage. Ohio weavers came from Great Britain and Germany in approximately equal numbers; consequently, the fact that Jacquard-type coverlets produced there are divided between single and double woven points to a fusion of the two traditions."

• **Colors.** A coverlet's colors indicate little about its origins. Almost all of them were dyed using indigo, madder, or other natural dyes. The presence of aniline dyes may indicate a later date. Careful scrutiny, says Checklist compiler John Heisey, may also reveal whether dyeing was done at home or in the factory. Home dyeing may be more uneven, though it often was evenly dyed as well. Since the housewife could save money by doing her own dyeing, this was a common practice.

• **Spinning.** Home spinning of yarns, which were then brought to the weaver, was another way of saving money and therefore was also widespread, especially in the early years of Jacquard coverlet weaving (1825–1830). According to Heisey, factory spinning, which often looks more even, became prevalent in the 1830s and '40s, and was very widespread by the 1850s and '60s. Therefore, a coverlet made with homespun yarn may be older than one made with factory-spun yarn. But without backup data to support it, such an assumption would be unwarranted.

• **Explicit Information.** Even more important than the implicit qualities described above, are the pieces of explicit information which weavers often included in their coverlets—the family names (his own and the customer's), the place names, and the dates. Many of these are quite clear, but perhaps an equal number of coverlets bear legends that, like old novels full of archaic language, are not easy to decipher.

For one thing, weavers were not grammarians and they frequently misspelled town names, family names, and proper names (including their own). Furthermore, if a proper name or word didn't fit, the weaver might start it on one line and continue it on the next, leading researchers to read the two lines as separate words.

But perhaps the most common confusion occurs when the weaver's name is indistinguishable from that of the customer. Some weavers, like Salmon Lake of Fredonia, New York, wrote the words *weaver* or *woven by* above or below their names. Others simply recorded their names. John Heisey offers one clue to the perplexed: If the name is a woman's, it's probably the customer's, since few Jacquard coverlet weavers were female.

In addition to the difficulty in distinguishing between weaver and customer, another common stumbling block in coverlet research is the heavy reliance on oral tradition for information. Coverlets are often passed down in families, along with tales concerning their provenance. Until recent years the authors of books and articles on coverlets frequently had nothing but these stories to rely on and thus perpetuated many of the errors held by coverlet-owning family members.

You can hardly blame them. Back in 1912, for instance, when Eliza Calvert Hall (a pseudonym) wrote *A Book of Handwoven Coverlets* (Boston: Little, Brown & Company, 1912), oral tradition, a time-honored way of recording and transmitting history, was very much alive, particularly in rural areas where most coverlets were made. The stories Miss Hall recorded were difficult if not impossible to verify because coverlets were not considered to be scholarly subjects or grist for journals, diaries, or ledgers.

Unfortunately, writers continued to perpetuate many of the old wives' tales surrounding coverlets. The result was that until recently, the record so conveniently left to us by Jacquard coverlet weavers in the form of both implicit and explicit information was never adequately deciphered.

Books like Montgomery's study of Indiana weavers and the Checklist have started to change the picture. One of the great strengths of the Checklist, according to the Birmingham Museum's Gail Andrews, one of the book's editors, is that "we decided we weren't going to rehash any of the information we found in other books, unless it could be documented with primary resource materials." To accomplish that, all the information on a coverlet, whether obtained from a book or a do-

Above: Jacquard double-woven coverlet by Martha Hedden of New York, 1835. This dark blue wool and natural color cotton coverlet features a large, symmetrical design of alternating rose and thistle-and-rose medallions, interspersed with eight-pointed stars. Graceful blossoming branches form the inner border, while the narrow outer border is composed of repeated Greek key motifs. Some coverlets were woven in two pieces. Like this one, they were often woven in widths of 36 or 37 inches. Art Institute of Chicago, gift of the Chicago Historical Society. Below: Double-woven Jacquard coverlet by Gilmour Brothers of Union County, Indiana, dated 1839. Natural cotton and dark blue wool. The border pattern of houses, trees, and pale fencing is thought to be unique to the Gilmour family of weavers. The Art Institute of Chicago, gift of Dr. Frank W. Gunsaulus.

Above: Beiderwand Jacquard coverlet signed "John B. Welty, Boonsboro, Washington, County, Maryland, 1839." This colorful example, with a border of birds and roses, is woven of dark blue, red, and green wool, and cotton in both natural and light-blue tones. The Art Institute of Chicago, gift of Dr. Frank W. Gunsaulus. Opposite page: Jacquard coverlet of double-woven natural cotton and blue wool, attributed to John Alexander of New York State, 1825. In this example, the word "Merritt" woven around the border may refer to the owner. A corner inscription reads "Agriculture and Manufactures are the foundation of our Independence July 4, 1825. General Lafayette." Note the masonic symbol woven between the border eagles. The Art Institute of Chicago, gift of the Chicago Historical Society.

nor, was double- and triple-checked against primary sources—for example, census records, newspaper ads of the period, court records, headstones, and weavers' account books. Not surprisingly, the man who compiled the information, John W. Heisey, is a trained genealogist. Of this unusual undertaking, he says, "Studying coverlets is really akin to genealogy, because you're looking for weavers; for people."

While the information in the Checklist is as accurate as modern research methods and care can make it, the book's editors consider it far from complete. Says Heisey: "A project like this is never finished. This book is only a start. A lot of research had already been done in Pennsylvania, Indiana, and New Jersey before we began the project. But there are other important states: New York, West Virginia, Illinois, and Ohio, for instance, that haven't been gone into very deeply.

"Furthermore," he continues, "we want to continue receiving information even on weavers we've listed because, in addition to knowing where and when a weaver worked and in what style, we'd like to get some idea of the volume of cov-

erlets he produced. We're also interested in finding Jacquard looms and Jacquard pattern cards. Of the 900 weavers in our book, we know that some 800 owned their own looms. They are still used in industry; but there is only one known Jacquard coverlet loom in North America today."

If you are interested in pursuing this kind of detective work, firsthand information has to come from the town or village where your weaver lived and worked. There he may have left behind an account book (a few have been uncovered and are housed in private collections and museums; others are very likely lying in attics waiting to be discovered). It's probable that the weaver who made your coverlet left behind a record of his affairs in the form of newspaper advertisements touting his services. He may also be listed in a census, although his occupation may not be given as weaver, since most weavers had other jobs to supplement their incomes.

The dedicated sleuth with the time and a bit of luck may be able to dig out this information, as Heisey and his colleagues did. But recognizing that most people don't have that kind of time, or the materials to mount such a search, Heisey suggests that coverlet owners send their information along with a photograph to the Checklist Project, Abby Aldrich Rockefeller Folk Art Center, Drawer C, Williamsburg, Virginia 23185. Other museums with large collections of coverlets, such as the Smithsonian Institution's division of textiles and local historical societies with an active interest in coverlets, help with such research as well. At these centers the facts about your coverlet, along with thousands of other threads of information, may one day be woven into a seamless record of 19th-century Jacquard weaving and weavers. ∎

How To Distinguish Weaver From Customer: A Case History

An illustration of the difficulty in distinguishing weaver from customer became evident during research for this article. Joel Kopp, a New York antiques dealer and proprietor of America Hurrah, brought out a coverlet he was offering for sale. The legend in one corner read:

Be ye kind and true
as youd have others be to you
and neither say or do to them
what e'er thou would not take again.
OHIO 1839 by A Allen.

A few days later, a perusal of *Hand-woven Coverlets in the Newark Museum*, a 1947 catalogue written by the late Margaret E. White, revealed an identical coverlet, differing only in the date—1842, in this case. A puzzling description on the facing page began: "A. Allen of Ohio was the mother-in-law of the donor. Unquestionably this coverlet was made for her by a professional weaver. . . ." The description concludes: "It is tantalizing to know that this skilled craftsman was in Ohio in 1842 and yet have no idea of his name. He would have been justified in signing his name to this coverlet as an artist signs any work of art."

This description contradicted Joel Kopp's assump-

tion that A. Allen was the weaver, *not* the coverlet's owner, and the words *by A Allen* woven into the coverlet would certainly support that belief. A check of Mrs. White's unpublished notes, dated 1954, showed that she had in fact acquired additional information on the coverlet, but had never gotten around to revising the published catalogue listing.

Her notes read, in part:

"A Allen was a professional weaver of Hillsboro, Highland County, Ohio. Since the Museum did its catalogue of hand-woven coverlets in 1947 four other bedspreads woven by A. Allen have come to light. The earliest of these is unsigned, but 1839 Ohio is woven in the corner. This coverlet is owned by the Art Institute of Chicago and is attributed to A. Allen because of its design. The border shows the same wavy lines and little birds used by Allen in later coverlets bearing his name. The ground pattern is a stiff repetition of flowers or stars, almost identical with an 1840 coverlet made by A. Allen. The latter has been preserved in the same family for three generations. It was one of five coverlets made for each of the children of a Quaker family living near Wilmington, Ohio."

White Quilts

U*ncluttered by colors, textile prints, and appliqués, white quilts offer an excellent opportunity to study the techniques and motifs of quilting.*

BY MADELINE ROGERS

Quilt enthusiasts, it has been said, fall into two groups: those who are primarily interested in the quilt's overall design—the quilt as art—and those whose primary fascination is with the workmanship of the quilt—the quilt as craft.

Collectors and *aficionados* of the second type find endless pleasure as well as food for thought and study in a group of quilts that one expert has termed "the quilter's final exam." These are the intricately stitched all-white quilts made primarily in the Eastern states in the latter half of the 18th century and first half of the 19th century by the most highly skilled needlewomen of the day.

Unlike more familiar patchwork (pieced) quilts, white quilts were not made for daily use, but as gifts, for show or for decoration. While we know so little about those who made quilts, it is believed by some that the women who made white ones had honed their skills in the making of perhaps dozens of quilts before they attempted an all-white masterpiece.

Because they were special—many white quilts were made as bridal gifts—scraps were eschewed and the quilt top was made of one large or two or three smaller pieces of white cotton (somewhat of a luxury in those days). The underside was cotton, sometimes of a coarser weave, and the interlining, when used, was carefully cleaned cotton or wool.

The lineage of the all-white quilt and its techniques can be traced back directly to ancient coverlets and quilted garments made the same way. The actual age of the technique of quilting—the joining of fabric layers using a small running stitch or backstitch—will never be known, but it is estimated by Thelma R. Newman in her book *Quilting, Patchwork, Applique, and Trapunto: Traditional Methods and Original Designs:* "Whether quilting . . . originated in Egypt. Persia, India or China, the Crusaders found it and brought it back to Europe and to the British Isles in the 11th and 12th centuries. It took 2,000 years to reach Europe."

In addition to the technique of quilting, makers of American white quilts employed several other ancient techniques to join and decorate their quilts. Two of the most popular were cording and stuffing.

To produce corded designs, layers of fabric were joined with parallel lines of tiny stitches—anywhere from six to 20 per inch. Then a soft cord was threaded between the lines of stitching to give a raised effect.

Opposite: Stuffed-work coverlet by Lucy Foot of Colchester, Connecticut, ca. 1816, cotton, 90″ x 87¾″. Almost as rare as a white quilt is a quilt whose maker is known. On this page (middle) is a detail of the centerpiece. Courtesy Stamford Historical Society, Inc., Stamford, Connecticut. Below: white stuffed-work coverlet. New England, ca. 1820, cotton, 77″ x 72″. A background of fine parallel lines contrasts the curved feather motif used throughout the design. Courtesy the Greenfield Village and Henry Ford Museum, Dearborn, Michigan. Above: White coverlet with fringed border, 18th century. In this design, the stuffed work lends a ripe appearance to the fruit. Courtesy America Hurrah Antiques, New York City.

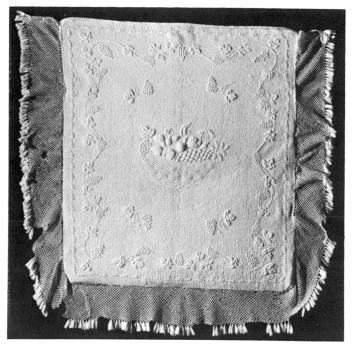

"Some Quiltmakers did as much with a needle and thread and a piece of white homespun as others did with all the colors, fabrics, and shapes of pieced quilts."

Patsy and Myron Orlofsky in their book *Quilts In America* state that cording ". . . is centuries old." It appears on the famous Sicilian Quilt—a very early 15th-century masterpiece that tells the story of Tristan in stitchery.

On white quilts, cording was often used to depict flower and fruit stems, create backgrounds and borders, and simulate the texture of basketry. The Orlofskys write that "there are examples of vases and baskets worked in outlines raised in fine cord on the early English counterpanes. These are surely the direct antecedents of the American quilts and counterpanes [made more than 100 years later] whose centers are these very baskets created from outlines of corded quilting." (Counterpanes are bed covers.)

Stuffed work is created by poking tiny wisps of cotton into prestitched designs to obtain a three-dimensional effect; it is also found on the Sicilian Quilt.

(Although this is not the place for an in-depth study of quilting terminology, it should be mentioned that stuffed work is sometimes called *trapunto*. However, since most quilt experts seem to object to this complicated European term to describe American quilts, the preferred terms *stuffing* or *stuffed work* are used here.) Stuffed work is prevalent, not only in white quilts, but also on the plain blocks and borders of appliquéd and pieced quilts. The quilter started by outline-stitching her design onto the two- or three-layer white background. The tiny stitches served a dual purpose: they held the fabric layers together and decorated the quilt's plain surface. As in all quilting, the stitches had to penetrate the quilt's top, lining, and backing and had to be so even that the quilt's underside was nearly indistinguishable from the top.

After the outline of the design was finished, the quilter turned over the coverlet and, using a sharp stiletto, gently pushed apart the threads of the backing fabric. Through the tiny aperture made by the stiletto, she poked wisps of cotton. (To aid the process, quilters often chose loosely woven cottons to back white quilts.) When the motif was solidly packed with stuffing, the separated threads were carefully pushed back together. Once the quilt was washed, the slight shrinkage of the fibers would normally obliterate evidence of the stiletto's work. In fact, the backings of many stuffed quilts show evidence of its entry point, and in some quilts, tiny "tails" of stuffing poke through the backing.

Completed stuffing creates the effect of bas-relief in fabric. A cluster of grapes tightly packed with cotton imitates the plumpness of ripe fruit; a feather-motif border encloses a central medallion not only linearly but dimensionally. To enhance the sculptural quality of the quilt, after stuffing and cording was completed, the quilter often stitched the entire background using a small-scale, all-over background pattern. Closely spaced diamonds and thimble-sized rounds were two popular designs. This would serve to compress the background, bringing the stuffed and corded work into greater relief. In judging the quality and beauty of a white quilt, the contrast of textures and levels created in this manner is one of the prime criteria.

Because they are uncluttered by colors, textile prints, and appliqués, white quilts offer an excellent opportunity to study not only the techniques of quilting, but the motifs as well, many of which were also used on pieced and appliqué quilts.

Where did these motifs come from? Experts have a variety of explanations, ranging from the historic to the fantastic. But, cautioned Patsy Orlofsky, in a recent interview, "You can't get carried away looking for the origins or meaning of motifs, because you see the same ones repeated over and over again in primitive arts all over the world."

For example, "The meandering line," writes Thelma Newman, "along with the spiral and the circle, as quilting patterns, are about 2,000 years old, whereas the diagonal line and lozenge design are said to be at least 6,000 years old."

According to Mavis Fitzrandolph's book *Traditional Quilting, Its Story and Practice*, many ancient quilting patterns used in American quilts arrived on our shores from England: ". . . a number of well-known English and Welsh patterns . . .

Opposite: Crib quilt by Rachel Smith, ca. 1870, muslin and cotton fringe, 60 x 35½. This quilt is dominated by a wreath of stylized flowers encircled by a bead-like ring. Courtesy The Newark Museum, Gift of Mary Elizabeth Morris and John B. Morris, Jr. Below: Stuffed-work coverlet, ca. 1810, cotton, 25 x 85. Like most white quilts, this was probably originally created as a wedding gift. While little is known about the women who made these quilts, it is believed that they honed their skills on perhaps dozens of patchwork quilts before attempting an all-white masterpiece. Left: Detail of quilt shown below reveals the geometric pattern stitched in the background contrasted with the sculptural quality of the stuffed grape and grape leaves. Helga Photo Studio, courtesy Rhea Goodman: Quilt Gallery, Inc.

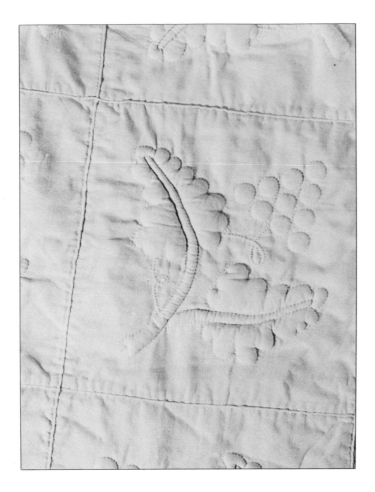

have been used [in America] again and again. Various feather patterns, including ring, wreath, running feather, several versions of the *twist* (called *rope*), *wine-glass* (called *teacup quilting*) the rose or whorl and of course *diamonds* (called *crossbar quilting*) were . . . popular."

Simple patterns, which in the skilled quilter's hands were transformed into works of sublime beauty, often had almost laughably humble origins, as these stories, recorded by Fitzrandolph, illustrate: "An instance of a new unit [pattern] designed . . . from a common object is given by Mrs. Bell's mother who, wanting something to fill a space on a quilt, made a template from the clothes brush and used this twice, one shape across the other. Miss Shepherd designed a pattern unit from the embossed leather binding of the family Bible. . . . The stamped pattern on the wooden seat of an ordinary chair gave her an idea for a new filling in her *shell* template. The moulding on the oven door suggested to Mrs. Davison's mother an effective all-over pattern."

Nature was another, more obvious, source of inspiration for the quilter. Leaves, feathers, flowers, and, less often, animals, have always been popular quilting designs.

In the case of American white quilts, these old traditional patterns were joined by motifs borrowed from the popular decorative arts of the day. The influence of the English architects William and Robert Adam, which seeped into every area of American decorative arts in the early 19th century, is clearly seen in white quilts with their strong symmetry and classical motifs. This is most clearly evident in the way the

white quilt was laid out: The majority have a central medallion enclosing a cornucopia, basket, vase or urn of flowers. Around this central section there is almost always a single or double border.

In addition to this symmetrical arrangement, the subjects are a sign of the times. They are often classically inspired, as were the designs of the Adam brothers. For instance, urns, lyres, and swag borders, obviously borrowed from the architecture and interiors of the day, abound.

To many experts, including Philip Curtis, curator of decorative arts at the Newark (New Jersey) Museum, this fact, along with other indicators—the time-consuming labor and inherent impracticality of the white quilt—point to upper-class origins. "These quilts are much less 'folkie' than other types," he says. "It seems as though the people who made them were the sort who kept up with the fashions of the times."

Even a devotee of the craft of white quilts, like Patsy Orlofsky, finds the sameness of the designs one of the strikes against these coverlets: "If anything disappoints me about white quilts it's the similarity of motifs. I find less whimsy in the all-white quilts than I find in pieced quilts. I feel more often than not that I'm looking at a variation on a theme the woman had seen; not at something original.

"The making of a white quilt, however," she continues, "with its exacting workmanship, is not the kind of activity in which fancy takes flight. It's possible that a woman with the kind of temperament and skill to do such work was not a very

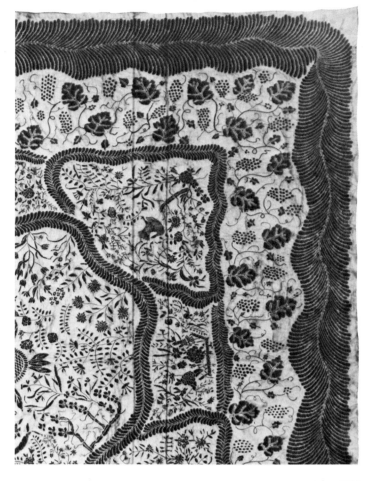

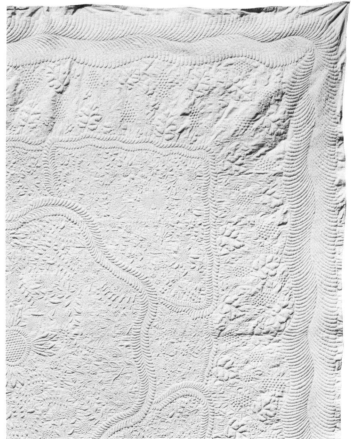

whimsical sort of person."

Because the designs of so many white quilts fall into predictable patterns, the rare ones that depart from the mold are highly prized. Thomas Woodward, the New York quilt dealer, advises collectors that a white quilt that strays from the norm is the one to look for. "Motifs that relate to historical events or to personal incidents are best."

An example was sold recently by Joel and Kate Kopp of New York's America Hurrah. The quilt, probably made in Vermont, circa 1850, consists of several squares of white cotton sewn together. Each square has been worked in a different design, in the style of a pieced album quilt. The price of the quilt, sold to a private collector, was "in the low four figures."

White quilts of any description are rare at any price for several reasons: First, their age. Most are between 150 and 200 years old. Even well-preserved pieced quilts of that vintage are somewhat rare. Second, because of the exquisite workmanship and time (estimated at six months to two years) to complete a white quilt, and the impracticality of keeping the coverlet clean, they were never made in abundance. Third, because of the fragility of the stuffed work, many of them have deteriorated badly, the tightly packed stuffing forcing itself in time through the quilt's top or back. Fourth, Philip Curtis explains that to get white quilt tops white, they were often bleached, sometimes more than once, weakening the fabric before the quilt was even stitched. And finally, many dealers are not interested in any quilt that is not in nearly perfect condition and of outstanding artistic merit.

Collectors, however, such as Orlofsky, have a different viewpoint and feel that even slightly damaged white quilts are worth buying for what they can teach us about the craft of quiltmaking.

Orlofsky collects them and other white quilted pieces—dresser scarves, pillow shams, and garments—because "I think they're the most beautiful. After seeing thousands of quilts, as I have, it's amazing to realize that a needlewoman could do as much with a needle and thread and a piece of white homespun as others did with all the colors, fabrics, and shapes of pieced quilts."

More than a pieced quilt, a white quilt with its thousands of tiny stitches tracing delicate patterns across a chaste white background thrills us with its intricacy and suggestion of countless hours of labor at the quilting frame. But even as we admire, we pause and wonder why anyone would undertake to make something that exacting. Many of us tend to dismiss such activities as tedious, compulsive, or even pathological, but that's a judgment that comes from an age more attuned to voracious consumption than to painstaking production.

Marie Webster, author of *Quilts, Their Story and How to Make Them*, wrote in 1915, when quilts were still being made by hand: "On quilts that were made because of genuine interest [and this certainly applies to white quilts, which could never be considered a practical necessity] the most painstaking efforts are put forth; the passing of time is not considered; and the belief of the majority of such quilt makers, though unconfessed, doubtless, is the equivalent of the old Arab proverb that 'Slowness comes from God, but hurry from the devil.'" ■

Pennsylvania German Quilts

In 1720, William Penn promised religious free-dom to radical religious groups—the Amish and the Mennonites—that had been relentlessly perse-cuted in Europe for years. They congregated in ru-ral Pennsylvania communities and provided us with an enduring legacy—their masterful quilts.

BY RUTH AMDUR TANENHAUS

Among the early settlers of colonial America, the Mennonites and Amish are perhaps best remembered—and are still ac-claimed—for their quilts. To appreciate this remarkable leg-acy, it is essential to understand the social conditions that played upon their religious lives as Anabaptists in 16th-cen-tury Europe.

The Anabaptists were regarded as radical left wing, consti-tuting a threat to both Catholics and Protestants. Their lead-ers were tortured, drowned, and burned at the stake with such relentlessness that by the close of the 16th century nearly all Anabaptists in Switzerland and Germany had been extermi-nated. Nevertheless, the movement spread through central and western Europe. In Holland, a Catholic priest, Menno Si-mons, abandoned the church to join the hunted Anabaptists. His followers became known as Mennonites. Soon, however, friction developed among the Mennonites. The principal source of contention was the interpretation of the *Meidung*, the practice of shunning a church member who had sinned. While most Mennonites believed that a sinner should be pun-ished only by being denied communion, one fiery and aggres-sive bishop, Jacob Amman, advocated that he or she also should be shunned totally by family and community. The controversy widened, and in 1697 Jacob Amman broke away from the Mennonites. Amman's followers became the Amish. Throughout this period, the religious persecution of all Ana-baptists continued.

It is small wonder, then, that when William Penn promised

these German sects—both essentially plain people, adhering strictly to religion and to an agrarian way of life—protection from religious persecution and inexpensive farmland in colo-nial Pennsylvania, they readily accepted his offer. Their im-migration began in the 1720s.

They congregated in specific rural locations, establishing self-sufficient farm communities. This deliberate separation from the "English" world enabled them to continue their Eu-ropean traditions and maintain their separatist belief system.

The Amish

The Amish were fiercely resistant to change. Each generation shared identical aspirations. Their small, homogeneous com-munities were devoutly religious. The Amish were opposed to luxury; their clothing was simple, somber, and without pat-tern. There continues today an aversion to electricity, jew-elry, and power-driven machinery of any kind.

The Amish simply do not conform to the world as we know it. For example, they do not engage in war. Buttons on outer clothing are forbidden, as they connote military bearing: in-stead, clothing is fastened with hooks and eyes. (Nevertheless, notable exceptions did exist. Some Amish fought in the Revo-lution, and others, as they were opposed to slavery, fought for the North in the Civil War.) For their children, education be-yond the primary grades is forbidden. It is a time when girls should learn household chores and boys should master the art of farming—a time to insulate yet another generation from the outside world.

The Amish carry no insurance and do not erect lightning rods on their buildings. Should a structure burn, the commu-nity provides manual and financial aid to replace it. Although they pay taxes, they eschew politics and refuse government aid in the form of farm subsidies or Social Security benefits. Hardworking, peaceful, loving, closely knit, they care for each other; security comes from within the group.

Amish society is firmly patriarchal. But it is in this

The Amish and Mennonite quilts shown here and on the following pages display similarities and differences that have root in their makers' outlook on life. Of the two sects, the Amish are more strict. Even today they have an aversion to power driven machinery; horse-drawn buggies, such as the one shown here, are not an uncommon sight. Below: Trip around the world, Mennonite, ca. 1890. Cotton, 81″ x 81″. Courtesy M. Finkel & Daughter, Philadelphia. Photograph of Amish family in buggy by Stephen Elliot from *Sunshine and Shadow: The Amish and Their Quilts* by Phyllis Haders.

presently unfashionable respect that we can first begin to understand and to grasp the beauty and craftsmanship of the Amish quilt. The Amish women were (and still are) submissive and wholly responsible for the cleaning of their sparsely furnished homes, and for cooking, child rearing, and tending to their traditional gardens. Because the Amish women are enveloped in routine, it would seem unusual that the quilts they have fabricated are visually moving, even exciting. But the dramatic tension achieved through the manipulation of color and the placement of geometric forms in Amish quilts is due, in great part, to the religiously mandated conformity to an unbending life-style. As nonconformity was tantamount to

rebellion, and rebellion in turn led to ostracism by family and community, the Amish women had to look to an "acceptable" means of manifesting their repressed creative instincts. As Frances Lichten has suggested in *Folk Art of Rural Pennsylvania*, "Quilts . . . were an outlet for love of color and a release for nervous energy."

Although written records are unavailable, it is assumed that the Amish made few quilts before 1860. Some researchers believe bishops may have prohibited the piecing of quilts in their church districts. Instead, the women probably wove heavy woolen blankets. Robert Bishop and Elizabeth Safanda, in *A Gallery of Amish Quilts*, speculate that it was not

Opposite: School house, Mennonite (made by a member of the Ehst family of the town of Bally, Berks County), ca 1900. Cotton, 80″ x 80″. Courtesy M. Finkel & Daughter. Above: Fence Row, Amish (Lancaster County), ca 1895. Wool challis, 78″ x 70″. Collection Arlen Roth, photo courtesy America Hurrah Antiques, New York. Both Pennsylvania Amish and Mennonite quilts are known for their vibrant colors and their bold patterns. The Mennonite women, however, showed more whimsy in their use of fabrics and in their designs. The more traditional Amish held to simple geometric shapes and solid color. On their pieced quilts, Mennonites used calico and check fabrics and applique designs, like the school houses shown at left. Amish women made only pieced quilts, but they made up for the lack of applique in richly textured quilting. Note the use of wreaths, tulips and stars in the border and in the solid patches of the fence row quilt above.

All the quilts shown here are Amish except the two opposite at top, which are Mennonite. Early Amish quilts are almost all made of large, simple straightedged pieces; the smaller pieced formats emerged later. Use of the square varies from placement at center, which dominates the entire design, to the smaller patches found in the sunshine and shadow (top, left) and double nine-patch (opposite). The tilted square makes a diamond; rectangles laid together form the bars pattern, triangles set adjacent to each other form the sawtooth. Resplendent on all the Amish quilts shown here is the beautiful quilting—Quaker feathers, pumpkin seed flowers, roses, vines, wreaths, and tulips—stand out in high relief. Although the Mennonite quilt utilizes the simple shapes characteristic of the Amish, it is not wool, and does not use a traditional Amish design, nor does it have a wide border—earmarks of an Amish quilt. The narrow border on the outside edge is made of calico—a clue of Mennonite work. Top, left: Sunshine and shadow, Amish, ca 1895. Wool, 82″ x 82″. Courtesy America Hurrah Antiques. Above, top: Bars, Amish (Lancaster County), ca 1900. Pieced wool, 80″ x 78″. Courtesy M. Finkel & Daughter. Above, bottom: Sawtooth diamond, Amish (Lancaster County), ca 1905. Wool, 76″ x 78″. Left: Diamond in square, Amish (Lancaster County), ca 1915. Wool, 78″ x 80″. Last two courtesy America Hurrah Antiques.

Far left: Ocean waves, Mennonite, ca 1895. Cotton, 80″ x 80″. Courtesy America Hurrah Antiques. Left: Sawtooth diamond. Mennonite, ca 1910. Pieced cotton. 76″ x 76″. Courtesy M. Finkel & Daughter, Philadelphia.

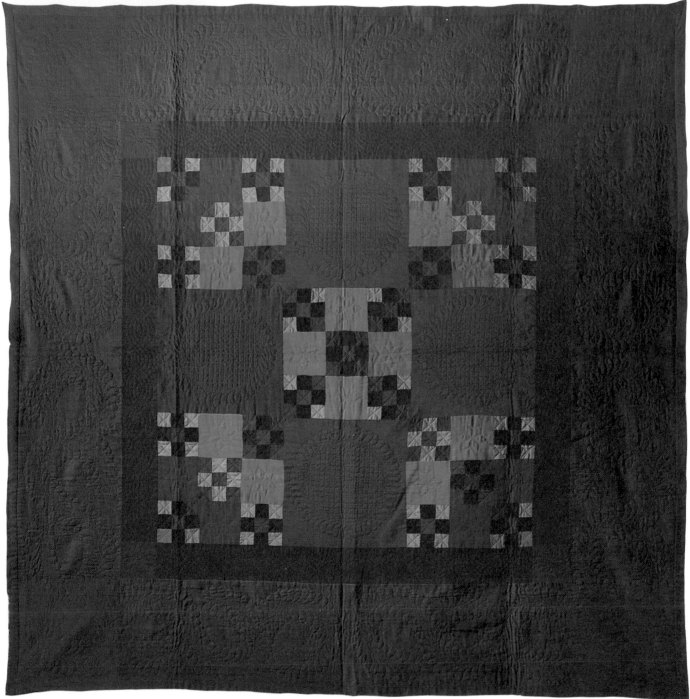

until the Amish had firmly established their communities, and had begun to socialize selectively with non-Amish neighbors, that they became acquainted with the "American" quilting traditions. Nonetheless, their simple quilts necessarily were adapted to their religious and social prohibitions and thus took on their distinctive style. The majority of the traditional quilts appear to have been made between 1870 and 1935.

It was customary for the Amish housewife—and in many cases grandmothers and great-aunts—to piece the quilt top at home. (A "pieced" quilt is one which has its top layer composed of swatches of material stitched together to form a geometric scheme of patterns and borders.) Amish quilts dating after 1860 were pieced by a foot-powered treadle machine. Once a backing was added, the machine stitching was not visible. After the quilt top was pieced, a filling, usually of coarse wool, was added for warmth. A backing material was then chosen, and the quilt was finally set into a quilting frame.

Templates or patterns were used to mark the quilt with the motifs to be stitched. Templates were made of a stiff material—cardboard, tin, or wood. The women traced around these patterns with pencil or chalk; some quilters dipped the templates in starch, creating a pattern on the top that later was brushed off. Some experienced quilters drew the motifs freehand, working without templates. Once the pattern was drawn, the quilter outlined the design with tiny running stitches. An accomplished seamstress could sew 20 stitches per inch.

The early Amish quilts were made of hand-dyed fabrics. The Amish quilter dyed her own cloth, mixing the dyes from native berries, weeds, and bark. The remarkably sophisticated Amish quilts dating between 1850 and 1870 are stunning because of the unique results achieved by the use of these natural dyes. Dye lots were never identical, and the Amish women produced myriad color variations. The materials for quilts came from used clothing and remnants from other sewing projects. They used every scrap from a faded lavender apron to a child's tattered pair of green trousers. Waste was unknown.

Amish quilts are characterized by strong, simple, geometric designs, often having the impact of contemporary painting. The motifs are composed of three primary shapes—the square, triangle, and rectangle. The use of the square may vary from a predominantly centered square, to smaller squares placed in the four corners, the tiny squares forming a double nine-patch or a sunshine and shadow design. Often a square is tilted so that it forms a diamond, and then the diamond may be adorned with triangles along its sides, forming the popular sawtooth pattern. Long rectangles are the dominant shapes in the dramatic bars quilt.

In Lancaster County, Amish quiltmakers generally favored wool made into center diamond, sawtooth, bars, sunshine and shadow and nine patch (or double nine patch) designs. Amish

women from Mifflin, Somerset and other Pennsylvania counties (as well as those in the Midwest) made quilts in a broader range of designs, often in cotton or wool and cotton.

Amish women were surrounded neither by elaborate textiles nor by wall coverings, nor were they familiar with the books and magazines that featured quilt patterns as early as 1840. What, then, was the source of their designs? Every Amish home had an *Ausbund*, the hymnal; it was bound in leather with brass bosses (relief ornamentation) to protect the book. Examination of the shape and placement of the brass bosses reveals a striking resemblance to many basic designs of Amish quilts. It has been suggested that Amish women, perhaps unconsciously, were influenced by the designs from these old volumes.

The Mennonites

The Mennonites share basic beliefs with the Amish, as both sects originally evolved from the Anabaptists. The Mennonites are gentle, hardworking, and devoutly religious. They share with the Amish the practice of noninfant baptism. They, too, feel that they are a people separate from the world, and they eschew worldly pleasures and sins. According to quilt collector and scholar Jonathan Holstein, the Mennonites—even when referred to as "gay Dutch"—are essentially plain people, and along with the Amish, are decidedly conservative. However, the Mennonites are more outgoing than the Amish and a bit more liberal. They worship in a central church building (the Amish practice home worship) and are receptive to moderate change. Thus, they will relate to outsiders, will utilize some modern technology, and are more tolerant of higher education.

In addition, the Mennonites were not subject to the strict church prohibitions that affected the Amish. Thus, the "gay Dutch" were permitted to experiment with new designs and color variations. Unlike the Amish, they were allowed colorful patterns in their clothing and vivid decoration in their homes. Corner cupboards and window seats were ornamented, chairs, dower chests, bride boxes, towels, crocks, jugs, hooked rugs, and quilts were adorned with colorful tulips, hearts, birds, and fruit. Birth, baptismal, and marriage certificates were illuminated with *Fraktur* art, a style of medieval manuscript writing with stylized foliage and scrolled letters, derived from 16th-century German prototypes. The fanciful and colorful motifs from their German background became the signature of the Pennsylvania "Dutch" folk art style. Pennsylvania Germans are often called "Dutch"—derived from *Deutsch*.

Amish and Mennonite quilts

The vivid, patterned, colorful patchwork appliqué quilts of the less conservative Mennonites are in sharp contrast to the simple geometric drama of solid, saturated coloration that

Below: Star of Bethlehem with princess feather, Mennonite (Lancaster County), ca 1800. Pieced and appliqued cotton, 85″ x 85″, ca 1880. Courtesy Thos. K. Woodard, American Antiques and Quilts. Left: Roman stripes, Mennonite, ca 1910. Cotton, 76″ x 76″. Both courtesy America Hurrah Antiques. A less rigid adherence to traditional form is evidenced in these flamboyant examples from the Pennsylvania Mennonite quilters who were slightly more influenced by other quilters around them than their isolated Amish sisters. While the Mennonites use the diamond shape as in the striking pieced star of Bethlehem below, it is combined here with the pinwheel shaped princess feather, appliqued in the corner squares. An Amish woman may well have stitched a design into the corner patches of her quilt using the princess feather motif, but to her quilt she would not have appliqued feathers or the tulips fitted between the alternating points of the star.

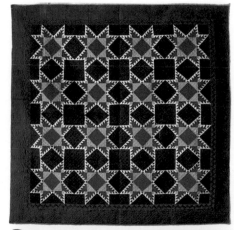

All the quilts illustrated here were made by the Pennsylvania Mennonites. They are distinguished by a vibrant use of color, as are the coverings of their neighbors the Pennsylvania Amish. However, there are features that distinguish them from the Amish—the applique on the oak leaf quilt (top, left), the use of white in the kaleidoscope (bottom, left), and the feathered star (above, top), the use of circular shapes in the pinwheel crib quilt (above) and the use of calico in the delectable mountain (opposite page, left). The Jacob's coat (opposite, right) was a popular Mennonite design, seldom, if ever, used by the Pennsylvania Amish. Top, left: Oak leaf, Mennonite, ca 1880. Applique cotton, 78″ x 78″. Left: Kaleidoscope, Mennonite (Lancaster County) ca 1880. Cotton, 76″ x 76″. Both courtesy Barbara S. Janos, Barbara Ross Collection, New York. Above, top: Feathered star, Mennonite, ca 1895. Cotton, 80″ x 80″. Above, bottom: Pinwheel, Mennonite crib quilt, ca 1890. Wool, 36″ x 37″. Both courtesy America Hurrah Antiques.

"The Mennonites, even when referred to as 'gay Dutch,' are essentially plain people. Along with the Amish, they are decidedly conservative, though more outgoing and a bit more liberal."

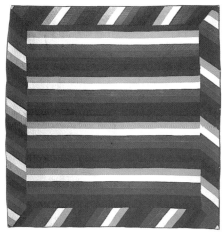

Opposite, left: Variant delectable mountain, Mennonite, ca 1895. Cotton, 64" x 64". Courtesy America Hurrah Antiques. Above: Joseph's coat, Mennonite, ca 1900. Pieced cotton, 72" x 74". Courtesy M. Finkel & Daughter.

characterizes Amish quilts. (An appliqué quilt is one whose top is of a whole cloth. Forms cut from other fabrics of contrasting color are then applied, or stitched down.) The gay folk decoration of the Pennsylvania Dutch—flowers, birds, peacocks, hearts—were cut from chintz, calico, and other printed fabrics. The names of the patterns are as gay as the motifs; cherry spray, seven stars, tree of paradise, turkey tracks, and drunkard's path.

An additional comparison between the quilts of the two sects is noteworthy. If the Amish-stitched motifs were replaced by appliqués, the Amish quilts would resemble the gay Mennonite quilts. Instead, the Amish quilts are covered with intricately stitched designs, all done by hand. Common quilting patterns are diamond grids, tulips, roses, feathers, and wreaths. And most Amish quilts have a wide, monochromatic border decorated with stitched feathers, tulips, or baskets. Thus, the intricate and superb Amish stitching was a permissible way of incorporating Mennonite-type designs without violating the *Ordnung*, their rules of conduct.

Perhaps the most gratifying element common to the quilting of both the Amish and Mennonite women was the sheer joy they experienced while creating their quilts at a bee or frolic. An important social event, the bee satisfied the desire for social interaction. It is no better expressed than in Gertrude Huntington's *A Dove at the Window*:

> As they sit around the quilt frames, they have a fine time talking and gossiping. The women move around during the morning, so that almost everyone has a chance to talk to someone else. They discuss their children, the school, the young people, marriages, and pregnancies. As they talk, their fingers fly; sometimes as many as six quilts will be finished in a day. After a full, long morning, the quilts that are complete are taken off the frames and the frames dismantled so there will be room to eat. Then the numerous dishes of gaily colored foods are arranged on tables and everyone helps herself, "smorgasbord style."

The quilts of the Pennsylvania Germans have become highly prized and extensively collected. Yet, in their time, they were utilitarian objects. Women produced warm bedcovers for their families; quilts were simply an esthetic solution to a functional need. The women who made them had no sense that their works were, or would be, part of the mainstream of American art history. These quilts—with their superb stitchery and inventive interaction of color and form—are a testament to the Pennsylvania German culture that flourished in America, and to the women who created them. ■

Moravian Fancy Work

Through embroidery and other artistic hand-crafts, Moravian girls expressed thanks to God for the skills he gave them to create beauty.

BY KATHLEEN EAGEN JOHNSON

The Moravians, a largely German-American religious sect that settled in Pennsylvania and North Carolina during the 1740s and 1750s, earned a reputation for artwork distinctive in style and quality. The development of their ornamental arts in the early 1800s attests to this. The Moravians even taught special artistic skills in schools founded solely for the education of Moravian youth. Later these schools were open to the public, and between 1785 and 1840 the Bethlehem Seminary alone enrolled over 2,000 girls from 24 states and six countries. Similar schools were situated in Lititz, Pennsylvania, and Salem, North Carolina.

Although not always recognized as such, Moravian-style needlework and painting is found in museums, private collections, and antique shops all across the country. Art bearing the Moravian imprint left Pennsylvania and North Carolina with students returning home and with 19th-century tourists who purchased handmade souvenirs in Moravian communities. Thus, Moravian art created mainly by the teachers and students of the three schools spread nationwide.

Moravians were a simple-living, plain-dressing sect, so the emphasis they placed on painting and needlework might seem surprising. Yet mastery of ornamental arts was held in high esteem among the intellectuals in the sect; they considered such attainments part of a solid and well-rounded education. In contrast, some outsiders felt it appropriate that a young woman's education consist mainly of decorative accomplishments. This was thought attractive to her suitors. Many wealthy young American women in the early republic spent the years before marriage involved in activities no more strenuous than visiting friends, receiving callers, and dabbling in the ornamental arts. In Moravian culture ornamental arts did not function as "man-traps," since courtship was nonexistent. Their ornamental arts expressed thanks to God for the skills He gave them to create beauty. Friendship and loyalty were favored themes. The group hoped that the art produced at the female seminaries would remind outsiders that a refined life-style need not be wasteful nor dissipated.

Opposite page: Worsted work stitched on mass-produced grids, 1820-50. Left: Ebonywork candle-screen with floral border around an oval picture. Paint and gilt on wood, 1820-40. Bottom left: Page from a memory book of water-colors, 1830-40. All from Moravian Museum; photos Greg Johnson. Bottom right: Stitched memorial wreath of ribbon work, 1826. Adams National Historic Site, Quincy, Massachusetts.

Above: Themes such as *Love and Friendship* are common in Moravian art work. This watercolor is on a loose sheet of paper, but often they appear in memory books kept by schoolchildren. 1820-35; 5″ x 8¾″. Moravian Museum, Bethlehem, Pennsylvania, photo Greg Johnson.

Ribbon work

Moravians introduced the art of ribbon work to America in 1818. Ribbon-worked souvenirs from worldwide Moravian headquarters in Herrnhut, Germany, so impressed Bethlehem school officials that they instituted a course in this novel needlework. The Moravians incorporated two techniques within their ribbon-work creations. They fashioned three-dimensional flowers and leaves from lengths of ribbon and sheer silk crepe, accenting these constructions by means of embroidery with ribbon, silk floss, and chenille. *Mrs. Royall's Pennsylvania* (1829) described the art at Bethlehem:

> The young ladies showed me their frames with the unfinished work, which surpassed beauty. They have introduced what is called ribbon work, recently taught by a German lady. This is very ingenious, and has still a richer appearance than the common way with floss silk. The ribbon work is shaped like the floss, very narrow and curiously worked into flowers and figures of all sorts and shapes; it is richer and much easier done.

School officials, quite conscious that only female Moravian seminaries taught ribbon work during the 1820s and 1830s, publicized this fact through the creation of "monumental" framed needlework pieces. To give the public the best impression of needlework executed at the Bethlehem Seminary, one principal called on the ribbon-work instructor to create a masterpiece destined to be hung at the 1827 Mechanic Arts Exhibition in Philadelphia. But teachers did not make all the ceremonial ribbon work. The students presented a large floral wreath of crepe, ribbon, silk floss, and chenille to First Lady Mrs. John Quincy Adams. Mrs. Adams evidently cherished this piece of ribbon work, since she kept it after moving out of the White House.

Of course, not all ribbon work was made on such a grand scale. Students created smaller and less elaborate versions of the Adams wreath, sometimes embroidering their names or a biblical verse in the center. Others decorated dresser scarves, pocketbooks, and boxes with ribbon work. An easier and flashier needlework technique, ribbon work replaced silk-floss embroidery in national popularity after 1840.

Worsted work

Worsted work, also known as Berlin work, was another "addictive" needlework that captivated the Moravians and their students from the 1810s through the '30s. Although archival sources reveal many utilitarian artifacts made of worsted work, including hearth rugs, footstool and piano-seat

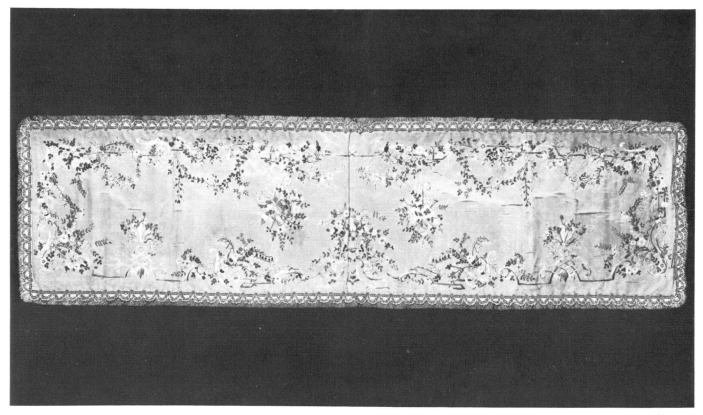

Above: Lyres and sheet music appear in this floral cotton embroidery. Silk on silk and cotton, 15⅜″ x 54″. Winterthur Museum; gift of Mrs. William Allen Jordan.

covers, table mats, and lamp and pitcher stands, only those objects created as pictures, framed and hung, survive in any numbers today.

At the turn of the 19th century, A. Philipson, a printseller in Berlin, Germany, invented gridded charts with designs on them corresponding to the holes in needlework canvas. By counting the holes and comparing the Berlin pattern to the canvas, a woman could re-create the Berlin work design in worsted wool. Even the colors of yarn were supplied on the pattern so the imagination of the needlewoman did not enter into "the picture."

Not everyone shared the nation's excitement over worsted work. J. D. Drinker, father of two Bethlehem schoolgirls, bitterly complained to principal Lewis de Schweinitz:

> I observe the materials for a Hearth Rug are charg'd $12, which is more than double the price I paid for a ready manufacturid [sic] one, now in my possession, similar in material, richness & variety in colours. . . . The attainment of the art of worsted working is perfectly useless, and the time employed in acquiring it more than thrown away.

The Moravians did not heed Mr. Drinker's advice. With the advent of mass-produced Berlin patterns, Moravian needlework lost its distinctive flavor. Moravian teachers or-dered commercially made patterns even though they were capable of creating their own and did so for several years. Caught up in the Berlin-work craze, the Moravians disregarded the loss of individuality in their needlework.

Watercolor drawing

Like worsted work, painting—or "drawing in watercolors," as it was known—was a very popular art for 19th-century women. Because elementary art instruction during this period consisted largely of copywork, students reproduced their instructors' paintings. This practice led to the development of stock Moravian motifs, including: stone monuments and urns, often topped by eternal flames or hearts, commemorating love and friendship; bluebirds with long, delicate wings, symbolizing happiness; circular horns entwined around sheet music; and puffy pink roses that look more like cabbages.

Two themes run through the paintings created at the Moravian seminaries: religious joy and the close ties among friends, which Moravians encouraged. The girls and their teachers celebrated Christmas and other holidays by painting and displaying watercolor religious scenes. They also kept schoolgirl memory books filled with painted remembrances, and exchanged decorated paper and silk watch papers, which

Above: The painted velvet lid on this distinctively Moravian work bag opens to reveal a pincushion. It was probably made in Bethlehem, Pennsylvania between 1820 and 1840. Silk, velvet, paint, and felt; 4″ x 3″. Below: The filigree work on the Moravian boxes and basket is done by gluing together bits of rolled paper. The lids are painted with watercolors. All date from 1790-1810; heart box, 2¼″ high; round box 2½″ diameter. All, Moravian Museum; photos Greg Johnson

Examples of watchpapers made and sold as souvenirs by the Moravians. These decorative and useful objects were placed in the backs of watches to keep the works free of dust. Watercolor on paper; 1⅞" to 2⅛" diameter. Moravian Museum.

were placed in the back of timepieces to keep the works free of dust.

Velvet painting and ebony work

It was a natural move for the Moravians to transfer their painting skills to surfaces other than paper. Account books and receipts indicate the purchase of velvet-painting materials as early as the 1810s, making the Bethlehem Seminary one of the first schools to teach the fashionable art in this country. From these materials schoolgirls decorated hand-screens, pocketbooks, and workbags. While much 19th-century velvet painting was accomplished through the use of stencils, the Moravians preferred to apply the paint to the velvet freehand.

Mrs. Royall pronounced in 1829 that ebony work, another form of painting taught at the Bethlehem Seminary, was "a very useful art and a great curiosity, everything almost is made of it." The art of ebony work resulted from the popularity of papier-mâché objects during the 19th century. To achieve the look of painted or inlaid papier-mâché, the Moravians devised a way of embellishing wood- and paper-based artifacts with paint, and in this manner they made work, shaving, and dressing boxes, writing desks, hand-screens, and mantle ornaments. Papier-mâché furniture often was painted

in elaborate rococo floral patterns on a black background or inlaid with mother-of-pearl on a black ground. In ebony work, which has nothing to do with ebony wood, the paintings often were done on a black ground to imitate papier-mâché furniture.

The exacting work of filigree is typical of the care Moravians took in executing their ornamental arts. After rolling thin strips of paper around a needle, the Moravians joined these little cylinders to construct boxes, both round and heart-shaped, and baskets, which were then decorated with ribbon and painted medallions bearing verses of love and friendship. Eliza Southgate recorded in her 1887 diary that the Moravian women sold paper baskets in the 19th century and that Candace Wheeler, the woman so instrumental in reviving interest in early American needlework, displayed a Moravian "paper box done with needle in filigree" at an 1883 fair to raise money for the Statue of Liberty.

The Moravians may have "shunned the follies of the fashionable life" but they practiced the popular ornamental arts with precision and skill and viewed this pursuit as a scholarly endeavor and a sign of a refined life-style. Through their mastery of ribbon work, worsted work, velvet painting, and the unusual arts of filigree and ebony work, the Moravians helped to enrich 19th-century American life. ■

Early American Splint Baskets

Native American tribes first made these baskets to store grain and carry food; later, decorated with natural dyes, the baskets were fashioned for sale to settlers.

BY JUDITH A. JEDLICKA

The decorated splint basket is one of the rarest, most prized, and most sought after of the old American baskets. Few have survived because the splints, thin strips of maple, hickory, or other hardwoods, have dried and broken after many years of use. Information about the decorated splint basket is sketchy. Researchers have pieced together facts—types of construction, materials, dates, and quantities made—from evidence found in digs, town records, newspaper ads and articles, and interviews.

Most American basket weaving and decorating techniques developed from traditions brought over from Europe and Africa by the early settlers. The decorating and dyeing techniques used on splint baskets, however, are strictly a native American art, originated by American Indian tribes living in what are now the states of Connecticut, New York, Mas-

sachusetts, New Jersey, Pennsylvania, New Hampshire, Maine, and eastern Canada. The bulk of the decorated splint baskets were made by the Mohegan, Scaticock, Pequot, Nipmuc, Massachuset (Natick), Montauk, and Western Nehantic tribes in Southern New England and Long Island; the Mahican of the Hudson Valley; the Iroquois and Mohawks of upper New York State and Canada; the Delaware and Munsee of Pennsylvania, New Jersey, and New York; the Pennacook of New Hampshire; St. Francis Abnaki, Penobscot, Passamaquoddy, and Malecite of Maine and Canada; the Algonquin of Canada; and the Massachusetts Mission Indians of Massachusetts.

Most splint baskets made by native tribes before 1850 were woven of handmade splints about three-quarters of an inch to one inch in width. Generally, the baskets were woven on the same size splint throughout and were either square or rectangular in shape. About 1850, Indians began to use gauges to make splints and molds upon which they shaped baskets. The gauge enabled the makers to weave baskets of relatively narrow splints about a quarter of an inch in width. This changed the surface area used for decorating. As more narrow splint baskets were made, fewer were decorated as they had been during the time of wide weave. By using a mold, basketmakers were able for the first time to make round baskets.

The first decorated splint baskets were made of ash splints about half an inch wide by the Massachusetts Mission Indians during the mid-17th century. This tribe was taught by the Reverend John Eliot to use a block print press. In fact, two

Opposite page, below: A complex weaving of different types of splints makes up the cover of the larger basket. It is decorated with the same motifs as the smaller basket. Courtesy Burton and Helaine Fendelman. Opposite page, top: Dyed and stamped basket made by the Onondaga tribe of New York. Above: Pequot, Connecticut, splint basket, 6″ w. The black stamped decoration on the wide splint has faded so it is barely visible. Both, Museum of the American Indian, Heye Foundation.

Mission Indians used this method to print the Bible in their native tongue. Sufficient evidence confirms that this tribe decorated splint baskets with blocks similar to those used for printing. They cut designs in tubers which they then dipped into natural dyes and stamped on the basket splints. There are no known extant examples of their work.

Most of the early decorations were made by stamping. The stamps were generally made of potatoes, turnips, and tubers. The design was cut into one of these roots, which was then dipped into a natural dye made from berry juice or boiled root. Stamps were fashioned in the forms of leaves, birds, flowers, and geometric patterns. Sometimes one design and one color was used on a basket. Other times, several designs and colors were used to create specific patterns. For the most part, a basket was decorated on all sides and on the lid, if it had one. Some rectangular baskets are not decorated on the fourth side. These were presumably intended for storage in a pantry where the undecorated side was to face the wall. The bottoms of baskets are left undecorated, but occasionally there is one design stamped in an outside bottom corner. The basketmaker probably did this to test the stamp before attempting to decorate the entire basket.

Why American Indians decided to decorate splint baskets in this way is unknown. The idea may have developed from the stamping technique the Northeast Indian tribesmen used to decorate their leatherware—shirts, pants, moccasins, pouches—and their bark containers. The leatherware patterns centered around animal life and geometric forms, however, while most basket designs depict floral motifs. The stamps used for leather and bark decoration were made of wood; the hard surface stamp made a clear print on the soft leather and bark. Conversely, for the hard wood surface of a basket splint a soft surface stamp was needed.

In the 19th century the American Indian began to teach his craft to white settlers, who went on to experiment with decorating techniques. In return, the Indians seem to have learned to make stamps of bundles of matches tied together, cork, bone, and the ends of mill spools. They also acquired

some free hand painting techniques, especially that in which a black outline is filled in with another color—much like a coloring book.

The first decorated splint baskets were probably made by Indians for their own use, chiefly to carry and store grain and food. Later these native Americans made baskets to sell to settlers. Oral histories tell of Indians who made baskets during the winter and sold them during the spring to townsfolk by travelling door-to-door or going to local markets. The Montauk Indians of Long Island made splint baskets of swamp maple, which they decorated by brushing the splints with pokeberry juice. Most of the Montauks lived primarily on fish caught off the shores of Long Island. By selling baskets they were able to purchase hog meat and winter provisions from the local farmers. The baskets sold to the settlers were generally used in the kitchen to store flour, grain, beans, and herbs; or to hold fruits, trinkets, and sewing. The more beautifully decorated the basket, the faster it sold and the more prominently it was displayed in a home.

Oral histories also indicate that substantial numbers of decorated splint baskets were made by the tribes in southern New England, but few examples survive. Throughout the 19th century, and as late as 1910, most of these baskets were made by the Mohegan and Scaticock tribes. In the early 19th century, the Massachuset tribe made large, round, and wide

splint covered baskets, each decorated with a barred blue circle printed with a potato stamp on a broad splint, dyed red. This was a popular form and a few examples exist in private collections. Many of the late Mohegan baskets were decorated free hand by using a stylus as a brush to apply color. The Scaticock makers developed a very distinctive type of decoration: a curlicue or roll, which was painted the length of one or more splints over the upright, perpendicular splints.

Sarah Crisco Sullivan of the Nipmuc tribe, developed unusual free hand designs painted with a brush that she fashioned of cow hair inserted in the end of a feather. She used beets and herbs for dyes. Her baskets were generally made of narrow splints in round and rectangular forms.

Eight basic block stamp designs were used by the Mahican Indians in the Hudson Valley to decorate their early baskets. The stamps were carved from potatoes and they were inked with natural dyes. Many of the later baskets made by this tribe were decorated free hand. Researchers believe that the block stamp designs of the Mahican and the free hand designs of the Mohegans were shared, and thus influenced each other.

The Iroquois and Mohawk tribes of upper New York State and Canada made wide splint baskets with beautifully colored block stamp patterns that were somewhat more geometric and sophisticated than those of the Mahican tribe. Often these patterns were stamped on brightly dyed yellow splints.

American Indian tribes developed the tradition and techniques of dyeing and decorating splint baskets, made of thin strips of hardwoods. Early decorations were done with stamps fashioned from potatoes and other tubers. Opposite page: Rectangular stamped splint basket. Courtesy New Jersey State Museum. Below: Splint basket with black painted decoration, made by the Mohegan tribe of Connecticut, who often used a brush or stylus, rather than a stamp, to decorate their baskets. Right: Tall covered basket of splints of varying widths, crafted by the Onondaga tribe of New York. Both courtesy Museum of the American Indian, Heye Foundation.

Two of the most popular designs used by the Iroquois were the feather and the new moon with a star motif.

The Philbrook Art Center in Tulsa, Oklahoma has some examples of decorated baskets made by the Delaware and Munsee tribes, including one basket made by a woman named Mawatees, who lived prior to 1836. She decorated her baskets by dipping a rolled coil of leather in dye and imprinting the pattern on a broad splint. Other basketmakers of the tribe made blocks of bone, cork, and the ends of wooden spools from local mills.

The Pennacooks of New Hampshire mixed broad and narrow splints in their weaving, decorating the broad splints with very simple designs. Some designs were stamped, others painted free hand. Examples of their work exist in the collection of The Peabody Museum in Salem, Massachusetts.

The St. Francis Abnaki, Penobscot, Passamaquoddy, and Malecite tribes of Maine and parts of Canada generally did not stamp their baskets. Instead, they swabbed the splints with colorful dyes. They tended to use a variety of splint widths in their weave and often added sweetgrass as a decorative element. Today they still make baskets in this style to sell to tourists.

The southern contingent of the Algonquin tribe created a very distinctive block print by cutting out portions of each pattern on potato or turnip stamps, in much the same way decorative rubber stamps are made today. Most were cut in flower and leaf patterns. Like the tribes in Maine and eastern Canada, the Algonquin still make baskets, although most are left undecorated.

Mackosikwe, also known as Mrs. Michele Buckshot, born in 1862, was an Algonquin basketmaker who learned the art from her mother. Records indicate that she made her potato stamp decorations with natural dyes. The yellow came from golden thread, the dark blue from spruce root, the red from blood root, and the dark brown from alder, butternut, or hemlock.

As many Indians learned to live in the white man's economy, the need for baskets—and therefore the art of weaving and decorating them died out. Thus today, the decorated splint basket has become a highly cherished piece in museum and private collections. ■

Opposite page, left: A Northeastern storage basket of ash splints, ca 1830, 9½" x 15". Opposite page, right: An unusually shaped basket of ash splints, ca 1940, 5" x 8" shows persistence of the craft to modern times. Both courtesy Museum of American Folk Art, photo by Carmine Fergo. Above: Rectangular splint basket and cover with painted decoration by the Mohegan tribe of New Haven, Connecticut. Courtesy Museum of the American Indian, Heye Foundation.

Bandboxes

Not *for collarbands only, these wallpaper covered containers served as the great American
catchall of the early 1800s.*

BY CATHERINE LYNN

As early as the 17th century, utilitarian, lightweight, wooden
or pasteboard containers were made in England to store linen
neckbands and lace bands worn by gentlemen. In 1755 Dr.
Samuel Johnson defined *band box* in his famous dictionary as
"a slight box used for bands and other things of light weight."
A wide range and variety of boxes, covered with wallpaper
and with papers made by paper stainers especially for such
boxes, enjoyed a peculiarly American popularity during the
second quarter of the 19th century.

The wallpaper trade in this country took these lowly
"slight boxes," enlarged them, embellished them with papers
that were block-printed in distemper and varnish colors, and
transformed their function. By the period of their greatest
popularity—between 1820 and 1845—*bandbox* had come to
have a slightly different meaning in America: a large
pasteboard or lightweight wooden box, oval or round in plan,
usually 12 to 14 inches tall, and covered with colorful decorated paper. The boxes served as the great catchall for America's overflowing paraphernalia of travel, for close storage at
home, and probably for the occasional storage of the collarbands from which their name derived.

Many bandboxes were the size of large modern hatboxes,
and some were indeed used for carrying and storing hats, as is
made evident by the labels of milliners pasted or printed on
some of these boxes. While to modern eyes they may all look
like hatboxes, bandboxes were put to numerous uses. A
printed handbill dated "Albany, July 28, 1835," now in the
Cooper-Hewitt Museum, provides but one among many bits
of evidence from the period that bandboxes were used to
carry almost anything. The handbill advertised a five-dollar
reward for the return of a "BAND BOX . . . LOST between the
Canal Bridge at Port Schuyler and the Patroon's Bridge." The
contents of the lost box were described as "Ladies and Children's Wearing Apparel."

If bandboxes were used by travelers during the second
quarter of the 19th century much as we use shopping bags today, they also were used by manufacturers and sellers of wallpaper just as stores today use colorful, eye-catching paper
bags to advertise themselves and their wares. Hartford paper
stainers of the 1830s emblazoned their names across their
products to bring them to the public's attention. Putnam and
Roff's colorful eagle grasps in his beak a banderole bearing
the partners' names and the words "Paper Hanging: Band Box
Manufac, Hartford Con."

Manufacturers of wallpaper did not produce bandboxes
merely as a sideline, however. By the late 18th century, a few
American craftsmen were devoting their efforts exclusively
to the making of bandboxes. One Widow M'Queen was listed
in the New York City directory of 1791 as "ban-box maker."
While other kinds of decoration might have adorned earlier
examples, by the 1790s wallpapers were certainly being used
to cover such boxes. Evidence of this is given in an advertisement of 1795 for "cheap paper hangings" including "some
. . . paper suitable for covering trunks and . . . bandboxes."

As early as 1800 Silvain Bijotat began to list his Bandbox
Manufactory in the New York City directory. In 1824, following his death, an inventory of his possessions was made. It
includes a listing, with evaluations, of the bandboxes left on

**Opposite: Bandboxes were covered with an almost infinite variety of
papers—some wallpaper, some paper made especially for these popular,
inexpensive containers. Note the classical, patriotic, and exotic scenes
decorating many of these examples on exhibition at the Shelburne Museum. Courtesy of the Shelburne Museum, Shelburne, Vermont.**

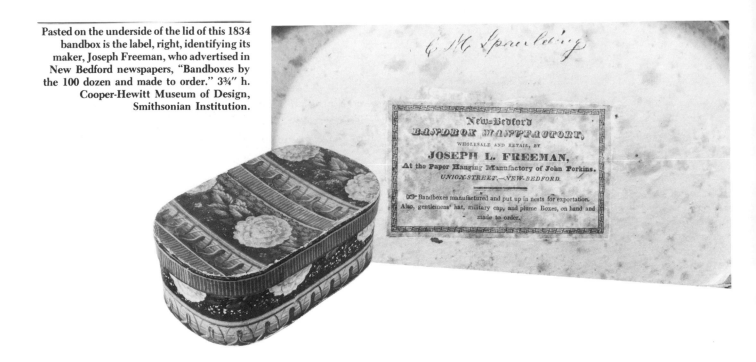

Pasted on the underside of the lid of this 1834 bandbox is the label, right, identifying its maker, Joseph Freeman, who advertised in New Bedford newspapers, "Bandboxes by the 100 dozen and made to order." 3¾" h. Cooper-Hewitt Museum of Design, Smithsonian Institution.

hand when he died. This inventory furnishes precise documentation for information implied in other sources—that is, that bandboxes were cheap and that "bandbox papers" as well as wallpapers were used in their decoration. The compilers of Bijotat's inventory made separate entries for "paper hanging," "band top paper," and "sides," as well as for "lining paper" and "Box board." Heading the list on the inventory are "2 doz nests of band boxes @ 7/[shillings, for a total value of] $21." These nests were sets of boxes in graduated sizes, which could be shipped packed one inside another, like Chinese boxes. Although it is not specified exactly how many boxes were included in each nest, there must have been at least three. Next on the list, ten additional nests received valuations of 5 shillings 6 pence each for a total of $6.87. At about $1.12 and $.70 for each nest, these must have represented handsome items. Even though these sums are not large, they do seem grand in comparison with other prices appearing in the list: some of the single boxes were assigned average values of only 2 or 1½ cents. Such low prices help to account for the wide circulation of bandboxes during the 1820s. The makers of bandboxes frequently pasted printed labels bearing their names and addresses inside the box lids. By comparing the information on the labels with newspaper advertisements and city directory listings, it is possible to pin down the dates during which a bandbox maker was working at the particular address. It is also possible to establish an approximate date for any wallpaper that originally covered the box. Since only one American wallpaper sample book for which dates can be documented has survived, and since there are pitifully few illustrations that can be accurately dated showing wallpaper patterns, bandboxes have proved to be particularly important sources of dates for patterns printed in this country during the second quarter of the 19th century.

Manufacturers frequently lined their boxes with dated newspaper. Although these can provide additional clues about the date of a cover paper and about the area in which it was used, one cannot assume that any dated newspaper found in a bandbox automatically establishes a date for either the box or its patterned covering. Because the bandbox maker could have used old newspapers, or because the box could have been relined long after it was first made, with then-current newspapers, or because the wallpaper itself may have been an aging, leftover scrap at the time it was pasted on, caution is necessary in attempting to establish just when the box and its paper were made.

As bandboxes became more and more popular, paper stainers began to print scenes on papers specifically designed to fit the proportions and shapes of the boxes. These papers were neither designed nor sold for use on walls. The designs were printed horizontally along a length of paper, as borders were printed, but each motif, though repeated, stood as a discrete scene, of the proper size to ornament the side or the top of a box; it was not visually connected by any elements of patterning to the next motif printed on the papers.

The New York business directory of 1840 included three lists of closely related tradesmen and craftsmen: "Band Box Paper Manufacturers" appeared as a separate, if small, category in addition to "Band Box Manufacturers" and "Paper Hanging Warehouses." Ten names appeared under the heading "Band Box Manufacturers." In 1820 only five names had appeared on a comparable list published in the directory for that year. The proliferation of these craftsmen during the intervening 20 years gives some indication of the growing popularity of their product. By 1840 there were twenty-five names under the heading "Paper Hanging Warehouses" in the New York directory. On that list ten names were marked

with asterisks, indicating firms that actually manufactured paper hangings. Of those ten manufacturers, two also appeared on the shorter list of four "Band Box Paper Manufacturers," three had duplicate listings as "Band Box Manufacturers."

The four New York manufacturers of bandbox papers whose names appeared in the directory in 1840 were Thomas Day, Jr., Archibald Harwood, J. H. Hazen, and George Peuscher. These men may well have been the principal sources of the colorful papers that appeared on the products of the much more numerous group of craftsmen who manufactured the boxes. Among them, these four may have been responsible for the scenes featuring New York landmarks that survive on numbers of bandboxes: Castle Garden—a concert hall on the lower tip of Manhattan, Holt's Hotel, the Merchant's Exchange, the Deaf and Dumb Asylum, and the lighthouse at nearby Sandy Hook.

Printers of bandbox papers apparently provided the same patterns to box makers in several cities. For example, one paper, commemorating the New York Fire Department's introduction, in 1830, of its new fire engine, No. 13, was used on bandboxes labeled by Philadelphia and New Bedford bandbox makers. Henry Barnes of Philadelphia used the paper to cover his labeled bandbox, and a duplicate paper was used by Joseph Tillinghast, a New Bedford wallpaper importer and bandbox maker, to cover the box bearing his label that is now in the Shelburne Museum.

A bandbox scene that has survived in large numbers depicts a chapel and what appear to be academic buildings, as yet unidentified. At Winterthur a bandbox decorated with this paper bears the label of Henry Cushing and Co., bandbox makers of Providence, while an example of the same pattern, differently colored, survives on a bandbox in the Boston Museum of Fine Arts bearing a label of Joseph Tillinghast of New Bedford. Many other examples indicate that in some cases there were common sources of supply for duplicate examples of these papers, while in other cases one paper stainer apparently copies another's pattern.

American landmarks of contemporary interest appeared on a number of bandbox papers made during the 1830s and 1840s. One on which the design incorporates the words "The Grand Canal" shows the Erie Canal, completed in 1825. Another shows the port of Buffalo. The new capital at Washington was depicted on another popular bandbox paper.

Coaching scenes and views of the new locomotive engines, of sailing ships, and of paddle-wheel steamboats probably were deemed especially appropriate for boxes used by travelers on the very conveyances they depicted. One printer gave his customers a "Peep at the Moon," shown as a pastoral landscape on a disk floating in a star-filled sky above another landscape on earth.

The subjects of some bandbox papers commemorated events that recently had captured public interest, like the balloon ascent of an Englishman, Richard Clayton, who in 1835 traveled 350 miles through the air from Cincinnati to Monroe County, Virginia. Bandboxes also played a part in political campaigns. In 1840 William Henry Harrison, presidential candidate of the Whig party, was the butt of a political joke illustrated on bandboxes. During the campaign, his opponents, the Democrats, contended that he was such a yokel that "upon condition of his receiving a pension of $2000, a barrel of cider, General Harrison would no doubt consent to withdraw his presidential pretensions and spend his days in a log cabin on the banks of the Ohio." The bandbox illustration shows the general greeting an old veteran in front of a cabin, with a barrel of cider on hand and the Ohio River in the back-

Architectural motifs frequently appear on bandboxes, like the one at right, rear, showing an unidentified academic building. 1820-40, 12½" h. Foreground: Note the typical oval shape of this 12" h. box, made in America between 1825 and 1840. Both Cooper-Hewitt Museum, Smithsonian Institution, the respective gifts of Mrs. Frederick F. Thompson and Alexander W. Drake. Opposite page, upper left: Wallpaper firms also sold bandboxes, as this advertisement from an 1829 women's magazine confirms. The New-York Historical Society. Opposite, upper right: The banner caught in the eagle's beak advertises the makers of this bandbox, George Putnam and Amos B. Roff. 1821-44, 12½". Opposite page below: The box on the left, 1829-44, 12½" h., commemorates a new pump wagon introduced by The Eagle Engine Company #13; while the bandbox to the right is covered with a geometric repeating wallpaper pattern popular in the mid-19th century. This cardboard example is supported by two wooden strips along the bottom, but some paper-covered bandboxes are made entirely of wood. All three the Cooper-Hewitt Museum of Design, Smithsonian Institution, given respectively by Eleonor and Sarah Hewitt, Mrs. Frederick F. Thompson, and Harvey Smith.

ground. (Harrison won the election, but died only a month after his inauguration.) Andrew Jackson, called "Old Hickory," and General Zachary Taylor, known as "Old Rough and Ready," also were depicted on bandbox papers.

Animals, exotic and familiar, ranging from bushy-tailed squirrels to giraffes, camels, and boa constrictors, were featured on one numerous group of bandboxes, as were fantastic animals drawn from mythological sources and many kinds of birds, including patriotic eagles.

Scenes from mythology were quite popular for bandbox papers. In addition, wallpaper patterns depicting gods, goddesses, and *putti* were appropriated for use on bandboxes. Since these were often depicted as self-contained decorative elements of a size appropriate for these boxes, many of them were used.

These were not the only kinds of wallpaper patterns frequently pasted on bandboxes. Hannah Davis of Jaffrey, New Hampshire, used repeating wallpaper patterns on most of the wooden boxes she produced between 1825 and 1855. Because their wooden construction was sturdier than that of pasteboard examples, bandboxes bearing her labels have survived in some numbers.

Wallpaper borders often were used to trim bandboxes covered both with repeating wallpaper patterns and with bandbox papers. Sometimes wide swag borders were used to cover an entire bandbox. In 12- to 14-inch widths, they were the perfect size for bandboxes. Swag as well as other kinds of borders in narrower widths were taken straight from the stock of paper decorations intended for walls and applied to these boxes. Tucked away as they usually were on closet shelves, bandboxes preserved numbers of wallpaper and border samples in unusually good condition and, with them, rare bits of documentation permitting dating of many of these patterns.

Although much has been written of their popularity among women who worked in the New England textile factories of the early 19th century, little has been published about the use of bandboxes farther south. Yet they certainly were sold and used in the South. This is made evident by advertisements like one that appeared in the *Daily Mercantile Advertiser* in Richmond, Virginia, for February 25, 1822. A "Mrs. White" advertised the receipt of "bonnets from New York" and the fact that she had for sale "BAN BOXES by the quantity."

By 1854, when Elizabeth Leslie published *Miss Leslie's Philadelphia Cookbook*, the moment of glory for the colorful bandbox apparently had passed. Miss Leslie, whose cookbook included advice and guidance on activities beyond the confines of the kitchen, wrote a brief section entitled "Travelling Boxes." In it she noted: "As bandboxes are no longer visible among the travelling articles of *ladies*, the normal way of carrying bonnets, caps, muslins, & c. is in small square wooden boxes, covered with black canvas or leather...." After that cutting observation, what stylish traveler would have dared to appear with bandbox in hand? Apparently very few, if we may judge from the dwindling numbers of advertisements for bandboxes and the shrinking lists of names given as bandbox makers in city directories during the late 1840s. The fact that the category for bandbox makers had been dropped from the New York City directory by 1850 is but one more indication that, as commodities in the wallpaper trade and as items of regular use by most Americans, they were fast disappearing.

Although stylish travelers of the late 19th century left their old bandboxes behind in attics, the name remained in currency. Connotations from the days of their glory survived in the still-used line describing the smartly dressed—looking as if they had "just stepped out of a bandbox." ■

PAPER HANGINGS, &c.
J. P. HURLBERT,
No. 222, Washington-Street, 2d door
North of Summer-street, Boston.

INFORMS his friends and the public that he continues to Import the latest styles and fashions of French Paper Hangings and constantly on hand a large assortment of American do. likewise imports fancy boxes of all patterns and sizes, fancy papers, &c.

Also, Manufactures Paste board boxes for packing all kinds of goods and for stores, and made to order of every dimension.

Also, All sizes Paste board Bonnet, Hat and Packing Boxes, Paste board Bonnet, do. Cane, &c.

The above named articles will be sold wholesale and retail on the most favorable terms, and sent to any part of the city free of expense.

Cast-iron Banks

For more than 60 years, cast-iron pigs, whales, and monkeys accepted the pennies of delighted American children. But mechanical banks represented more than a savings game; they were frank reminders of the social mores of the time.

BY HEIDI L. BERRY

Mechanical banks, those delightful toys that encouraged 19th-century children to save their pennies, are uniquely American. In the years following the Civil War, traditional American values of frugality combined with Yankee ingenuity to produce saving devices that offered entertainment as a reward for thrift.

An increasing number of collectors are as delighted today by the clever action of these banks as any child of long ago. The subject matter of the banks, viewed through the distance of time, provides insight into the social, political, and cultural milieu, as well as into the historic events and technological advances of the late 19th century.

The golden age of mechanical banks spans a period approximately 60 years, from 1870 to 1930. The first of these banks appeared at a time when cast iron, their basic material, was plentiful. So was inexpensive labor, provided by men skilled at handling the iron, as the intricate designs of many banks will attest.

No company was formed expressly for the manufacture of these coin receptacles. They initially appeared as accessories to already established hardware, tool, and toy businesses. Such a company was J. & E. Stevens of Cromwell, Connecticut, manufacturer of the first mechanical bank, and the most prolific bank manufacturer for over 50 years.

Other prominent early manufacturers included the Shepard Hardware Manufacturing Company of Buffalo, and Kyser and Rex of Philadelphia. The emergence of these companies, all in the Northeast, would seem to bear a more than coincidental relationship to the work ethic so integral a part of this Protestant area.

Patent papers, dated December 21, 1869, exist for the oldest mechanical bank, "Halls Excelsior," designed by John Hall of Watertown, Massachusetts, for the Stevens Company. This rather small bank is in the shape of a building. When the doorbell is pulled, the dome opens to reveal a delightful monkey, identified as "Cashier" by a paper label above his head. The weight of the penny, which is placed on the table in front of this unique teller, causes the dome to snap shut, taking the coin along with it. Perforations in the cast-iron walls of the bank allowed children to see their accumulation of capital.

This captivating invention was soon followed by more, designed by John Hall and others. The most prolific bank designer, as well as the most creative, was Charles A. Bailey. He began and ended his career working independently but spent the greater part of 40 years in between at the Stevens Company and is responsible for no less than 29 bank designs, the first of which was patented in 1880. Bailey's work is characterized by rich foliage, profuse flowers, and painstaking attention to detail. He favored a spring mechanism that caused objects, such as flags or figures, to pop up unexpectedly, resulting in an unanticipated element of surprise. In his most sophisticated effort, "Professor Pug Frog" (1880s), the strong spring mechanism causes the frog, which sits on a bicycle, to make a complete revolution as he deposits the coin. It is easy to imagine the squeals of delight this elicited from the young owners! The disadvantage of the spring mechanism is its fragility, one reason many of Bailey's banks are hard to find today.

Bailey was not the only designer working for Stevens. James H. Bowen of Philadelphia also supplied the company

with enchanting designs, among them some of the most desirable and complicated of all mechanicals, such as "Calamity" and "Girl Skipping Rope." According to a workman at the foundry, "Girl Skipping Rope" (1890) was one of the most difficult banks to cast, and this resulted in the wholesale price being raised to $18 a dozen. At that price, it did not sell well and, therefore, is among the rare banks today. A contemporary collector would pay $5,000 to $10,000, depending on condition, for this particular bank.

Manufacturers were extremely sensitive to the highly competitive market, and they utilized many areas of interest as subject matter. Some banks were directed toward very young children and took their inspiration from well-known fairy tales. Such banks as the extremely rare "Old Woman Who Lived in the Shoe" (1883) and "Little Red Riding Hood" had immediate appeal, as did the less rare "Santa Claus" (1889).

Contemporary children's literature was also a source for bank designs, resulting in creations such as "Uncle Remus," the storybook figure who was at the height of his fame in the 1890s. Comic-strip characters such as Buster Brown and his dog Tige also became the subject of mechanical banks, in this case under the title "Shoot the Chute" (1906).

Some banks were made to appeal particularly to little girls. Three early banks that fit this category, all very charming, are "Speaking Dog" (1885), "Confectionary" (1881), and the previously mentioned "Girl Skipping Rope." For boys, there was

American toy manufacturers produced some 250 mechanical banks to teach and entertain thrifty Victorian children. Above right and left: *Calamity*, 1905, designed by James H. Bowen for the J. & E. Stevens Co. The sportsmen huddle when a coin is inserted and the lever pressed. Courtesy the Seamen's Bank for Savings, New York; photos Mysak/Studio Nine. The Irishman is the subject of the bank at right: *Paddy and His Pig*, 1882. Bowen for Stevens Co. The New-York Historical Society.

Mechanical banks were primed with a coin or a button, and the show was on. Above: *Lion and Two Monkeys*, 1883, Kyser & Rex. A penny is set in the monkey's hand, a lever pulled, and the coin plops into the lion's mouth as the smaller monkey scrambles for a look. Below: *Novelty Bank*, 1872. Designed by Charles C. Johnson for Stevens Co. A cashier extends his tray expectantly; when a coin is placed there and the door closed, the man deposits the amount. Both The New-York Historical Society.

"Boy on Trapeze" (originally known as "French's Automatic Toy Bank"), an extremely delicate bank that performed according to the amount of money deposited. You got one turn for a penny, two for a nickel, three for a quarter, and six spins for fifty cents. Other subjects of particular interest to boys were the "Boy Scout" (1917) and "Boys Stealing Watermelons," both Bailey banks.

The opportunity to instruct through these banks and the resulting appeal to adults who were, of course, the purchasers, was not lost on manufacturers, who made a number of them with specific teaching possibilities. One of these, the "Picture Gallery" (around 1885), not only served as a bank but also taught the alphabet and counting.

Another educational and very charming bank, with special appeal for little girls, is the rare "Perfection Registering." A dime is necessary to operate this device, and as the coin falls into the bank, a little girl, accompanied by her pet cat, moves along a blackboard, noting with a pointer the amount of money the bank contains. Although no patent papers exist for this bank, the design is clearly that of Bailey. This attribution (and that of Stevens as manfacturer) is further confirmed by the recent discovery of "Perfection Registering" parts in the possession of a former Stevens worker.

Historical banks

The educational aspect of mechanical banks was not confined to counting and reading but extended to a wide range of historic events, including the discovery of America. The "World's Fair Bank" (1893), also known as the "Columbus Bank," was made by Bailey to commemorate the 400th anniversary of the discovery of America, an event that was also celebrated by the World's Columbian Exposition held in Chicago in 1893. Examples of this bank inscribed "World's Fair Bank" refer directly to the exposition and were, in effect, souvenirs. As this model proved popular, production continued after the fair, without the inscription.

Bailey restricted the use of color in this bank to gold, in deference to the commemorative role it played, and directed his considerable artistic sensibilities instead to an even greater degree of detail than usual. Columbus sits atop a tree stump, appropriately dressed in 15th-century costume, surveying a lush tropical paradise, complete with dense foliage and wildlife (in the form of a monkey). The base of the bank portrays the broad physical aspects of this vast country, a subject of special interest to 19th-century Americans. On one side of the base, Columbus's ship, the *Santa Maria*, lies at anchor in the deep harbor. On the other side, a mounted Indian pursues a buffalo over the grassy plain.

The action of the bank is intriguing. When a lever is pressed, the tree trunk in front of Columbus pops up to reveal an Indian chief, who extends a peace pipe as Columbus raises his hand in greeting and as the coin falls into the base.

Other historical banks referred to more contemporary events, such as the Spanish-American War of 1898. Two banks, "U.S. and Spain" (1898) and the rare "Admiral Schley Bottling Up Cervera," relate to this short-lived conflict.

Another contemporary historical event, the expeditions to

the North Pole in 1909, was commemorated by the "North Pole" bank (1910), designed by Bailey for Stevens. It came on the market at the height of the controversy between Rear Admiral Robert Peary and Dr. Frederick Cook as to who had reached the Pole first, and, diplomatically, did not portray either explorer. Instead, the design featured eskimos, seals, dog sleds, and other symbols of the Arctic. When the direction "Put Coin in Slot," written on the bank, is followed, an American flag pops up to fly proudly over the North Pole as the coin drops into the bank.

Political banks

Manufacturers of mechanical banks also took note of contemporary political events. The rise of corrupt city governments, a political reality in the last half of the 19th century, was portrayed in one of the earliest and most popular banks. Called "Tammany," after New York's Tammany Hall, where it first appeared as part of the political memorabilia of the 1872 Democratic Convention, it referred to that city's infamous "Boss Tweed," who was sent to jail in 1873 for embezzlement of public funds. The bank did not actually resemble Tweed. Instead, it depicted a typical politician of the times, a rotund and mustachioed figure, complete with bow tie, seated in a chair. After accepting a coin in his right hand, the figure immediately deposits it into the bank, as he acknowledges it with a simultaneous nod of the head. The action in this bank is precipitated by the weight of the coin, an appropriate if not intentional corollary to the crime it depicts.

After the turn of the century this bank was reissued without the imprint "Tammany Bank." Called instead "Little Fat Man," it still had great appeal, although its particular political significance had become part of history.

Patriotic banks

Another popular bank that is a favorite in almost any collection today is "Uncle Sam" (1886), made by the Shepard Hardware Co. of Buffalo, New York. It sold well and was used frequently, as evidenced by its relative abundance and generally poor condition. The figure is a typical 19th-century depiction of this American symbol of government. A tall man, complete with high hat, umbrella, and beard, stands atop a base, the front of which bears an American eagle, holding in its beak a banner with the words "Uncle Sam." If his dress of red and white striped pants, star-covered blue vest, and red and blue tail coat leaves any doubt as to his identity, the action immediately clarifies the matter. A penny inserted into the figure's hand drops as a satchel, marked "U.S.," opens to catch it, and Uncle Sam's beard and mouth move in realistic acknowledgment. Although there was no income tax at this time, other taxes made the figure as readily understandable then as it is today.

Religious banks

The Shepard Hardware Co. also designed one of the four known mechanical banks that have a religious subject, "Jonah and the Whale" (1890). The Shepard Jonah works on a principle similar to the "Uncle Sam." The bank is clearly identified by "Jonah and the Whale" marked on the base. Above, a

Above: The Shepard Hardware Co.'s *Uncle Sam* **bank is as popular with today's collectors as it was when first manufactured in 1886. The familiar Uncle Sam figure, with his high hat, beard, and umbrella, is ready to accept money. Place a coin in his hand and press the button behind his umbrella—the U.S. carpetbag opens and Uncle Sam drops the coin inside, acknowledging payment with a gesture of his mouth. Courtesy the Seamen's Bank for Savings; photo Mysak/Studio Nine.**

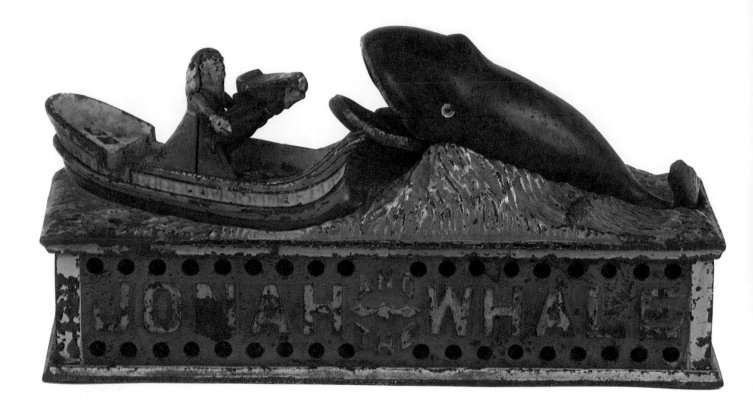

figure with long hair and flowing red robe, personification of God, stands in a boat, on a turbulent sea, holding the figure of Jonah in his hands. As the lever is pressed, the coin, which has been placed on top of Jonah's head, is propelled into the whale's yawning mouth as the God-figure pushes Jonah to his fate. The mouth of the whale opens and closes after the initial action, much like the Uncle Sam, an action which may have given the children who used it cause for thought as to the fate of this biblical figure.

This subject proved a fertile one for bank manfacturers, and another bank features a different aspect of the same story. Called "Jonah and the Whale on Pedestal," to distinguish it from the more common Jonah on base, this bank has no patent papers or advertising material, and therefore neither the date nor the manfacturer is known. The coin is placed in a holder, located near the whale's tail, and when the lever is pushed, the coin drops into the base, as the whale opens his mouth and deposits Jonah on dry land. This extremely rare bank was sold at auction in June 1978 and realized $18,500 to a Baltimore dealer, who sold it for a handsome profit.

The other two religious mechanicals, "Moody and Sankey" (1879), depicting the contemporary revivalists, and "Preacher in the Pulpit," are also extremely rare, suggesting that the union of religious and monetary themes was not one with which late-19th-century Americans were comfortable.

Ethnic bias

The great influx of immigrants to America from 1860 onward, from both Europe and China, quickly gave rise to racial prejudice, a sentiment vividly portrayed in mechanical banks, de-spite the fact that they were made as children's playthings and savings devices. Ironically, the banks which relay these biases are among the most charming mechanicals. As a group they are colorful, and the action is ingenious.

No ethnic group was spared. The Chinese, Irish, Jews, and particularly the American black—often stereotyped by late-19th-century society—were all utilized as subject matter.

Banks depicting the Chinese were among the most pointed in their attack. By 1880 there was considerable resentment against the more than 75,000 Chinese who had originally come as laborers to build the Transcontinental Railroad. So strong was the anti-Chinese sentiment that in 1882 Congress passed the Chinese Exclusion Act prohibiting any further entry of Chinese for ten years. That same year the "Reclining Chinaman" (1882) was patented by James H. Bowen of Philadelphia and manufactured by the prolific Stevens Co. An Oriental man rests against a log, a smile on his face, a long braid winding down his back and across his stomach. In his hand he holds playing cards. The rat at the base of the log gives the first negative connotation, an impression the action makes more forceful. When the lever is pressed, the penny, which rests on the Chinaman's hip, falls through his gown, into the base, as he moves his hands, revealing the cards, all of which are aces. The implication, that the Chinaman couldn't lose, paralleled the feelings of the white workingmen, who saw the Chinese as taking the only jobs available, at prices they themselves were unwilling to accept.

There are two other anti-Chinese banks, both quite rare: "Shoot That Hat" (1882) and "Chinaman in Boat" (1880s), suggesting the intensity of the anti-Chinese feeling.

Opposite page: *Jonah and the Whale*, 1890, manufactured by the Shepard Hardware Co. This is one of only four known mechanical banks with a religious theme. Right: *Circus* bank, 1889. Designed by Peter Adams and Charles Shepard for the Shepard Co. Clowns and the circus inspired a number of banks, including this example, which is unusual for its circular base and the use of a crank instead of a lever. Both courtesy the Seamen's Bank for Savings; photos Mysak/Studio Nine.

The Irish, who also labored on the Transcontinental Railroad, provided the subject matter for a bank, also by James Bowen, originally called "Shamrock Bank." Commonly known as "Paddy and the Pig," (1882), this colorful bank depicts an Irishman (clearly indicated by the shamrock and pipe on his hat) eating with a pig. The pig kicks a penny, placed on his snout, onto Paddy's outstretched tongue, and as Paddy swallows it, he rolls his eyes.

Jews, who immigrated in large numbers from Eastern Europe to the United States in the late 19th century, were also portrayed unfavorably. "The Bread Winner's Bank," which appeared in the 1880s, depicts the emerging struggle between business and labor. On one side of the bank, the head of a figure with Semitic features protrudes from a sack marked "Boodle, Steal, Bribery." Another figure, also with stereotyped Semitic features and a yarmulke, the head covering worn by Jews, holds a club marked "Monopoly." A coin placed on the club falls into a loaf of bread marked "Honest Labor Bread" as the laborer's hammer hits the club of monopoly, causing the stereotyped figure to flip upside down and literally enact the slogan marked on the bank: "Send the Rascals Up." This, of course, alluded to the penitentiary.

The delicate mechanism no doubt resulted in many broken "Bread Winners," and therefore this bank is difficult to find today. It is particularly interesting, as it combines the historic economic struggle between business and labor with ethnic bias.

By far the largest number of banks using ethnic stereotypes involved the American black. One of the most common types of bank, the bust bank, comes in no fewer than ten versions.

Although the names, including "Jolly Nigger" (1882) and "Uncle Tom" (1882), varied, all depict the stereotyped black man with thick lips, large eyes, and curly hair. With a push of the lever, a coin placed in the figure's hand is deposited into its mouth. This type of bank was very popular and was made in both England and France as well as in the United States. Today most banks of this style are fairly common.

More than 20 other mechanical banks utilize the same theme, portraying black people as the butt of a joke. One of the most colorful of these banks involves farm life, and suggests both the slower pace of 19th-century living and the stereotype of an ignorant and lazy black man. "Bad Accident" (1890s) bears the familiar Bailey foliage and is another Stevens product. A black man, eating a watermelon, sits on a cart pulled by a donkey. A large bush hides a little black boy. When the lever is pressed, the boy jumps out from behind the bush, frightening the donkey, who rears up and causes the cart to tip over and the penny to fall in.

"The Dentist" (1880s) again plays upon the racial prejudices of the times. Here the dentist is extracting a tooth from the wide-open mouth of his patient, a black man. When the lever is pushed, the dentist falls back, with the tooth, and the patient falls over backward out of his chair, as the strategically placed coin drops into the dentist's pocket.

Sporting events

However, not all banks that portray the American black reflect prejudice. "Darktown Battery" (1888), designed by James Bowen and manufactured by the Stevens Co., depicts

Above: *Speaking Dog*, 1885, Shepard Co. Several banks were designed specifically to appeal to little girls. Here a dog snaps his jaw when the girl drops a penny from her paddle. Below: *Horse Race*, 1871. Designed by John Hall for Stevens Co. When a coin is deposited and the cord pulled, the two horses fly gracefully around the ring. Both courtesy the Seamen's Bank for Savings; photos Mysak/Studio Nine.

the all-American game of baseball. The figures of pitcher, catcher, and batter are black. The coin, replacing the ball, is placed in the pitcher's hand, and when the lever is pushed, he throws it as the batter simultaneously swings, the catcher moves, and the money falls into the bank through an opening in the catcher's chest protector.

Perhaps the best-known hunting bank, of which there were many, involves a U.S. President and is called "Teddy and the Bear." This bank commemorates an actual event in which President Theodore Roosevelt, while bear hunting in Mississippi in 1902, refused to shoot a bear cub. This event inspired the now standard child's teddy bear, and resulted in a bank manufactured in 1906 by the Stevens Co. Roosevelt aims his gun at a tree, with the penny resting on top of the gun, and as the lever is pressed, the coin is propelled, by action of a spring, from the gun into the tree. At the same time, a bear pops out of the tree, surprising the President, and delighting the depositor.

Technology

The later 19th century witnessed many technological advances. Hailed as great achievements, they were not overlooked as subject matter for mechanical banks. It is ironic that the inventions, themselves created from extraordinary imagination, did not result in particularly imaginative or even interesting banks. The sewing machine, camera, telephone, trolley car, and X-ray were all commemorated by banks. The brightly colored "Trolley Motor Bank" moves forward and rings a bell when the coin is inserted; the "Telephone" rings when it is wound; the "Sewing Machine" needle moves, and a picture pops up from the "Camera" with insertion of the coin.

Most ingenious of the group is the "Smyth X-ray" (1898), patented by Charles Smyth of Dayton, Ohio. Through the use of mirrors, the bank gives one the illusion of looking through the coin, the very effect of the X-ray machine itself!

Although these banks accurately reflected the inventions, both in appearance and action, they lacked the color and excitement of many other banks in the marketplace and most likely did not sell well. Today all these banks are extremely rare and highly coveted by collectors.

Entertainment

In 1871 P.T. Barnum presented "The Greatest Show on Earth" in New York, and ten years later formed a partnership with James Bailey, producing the famous Barnum and Bailey Circus. The circus entertained almost every late-19th-century American and inspired a large number of very colorful and charming banks.

Clowns, certainly a major ingredient of any circus, figure prominently in these banks. The "Circus" (1889), a brightly colored and highly prized bank, features a clown in a cart, pulled by a small pony who realistically gallops around the circular base. A penny placed on a ledge is pushed into the bank by the clown's upraised hand as he passes by. This bank, patented by Peter Adams and Charles Shepard and manufactured by the Shepard Co., is of particular interest because it is one of the few designed with a circular base, and with a crank rather than a lever to initiate the action.

Another circus bank, the colorful "Humpty-Dumpty" (1882), features a performer who was active at this time. In the form of a bust bank, it is the most appealing of its type, and one of the most popular of all mechanicals.

Banks also documented other forms of late-19th-century entertainment. Country fairs are represented by the extremely rare and charming "Merry Go Round" which originally sold for $8.50 a dozen. Its value today is between $7,000 and $15,000 each, depending upon condition.

Puppet shows, another popular entertainment form, are represented by the most famous of all puppets, "Punch and Judy" (1884). Made by the Shepard Co., Punch and Judy fight, as usual, and their action causes the coin to fall into the bank.

Among other categories of mechanical banks are buildings, which provide a cursory view of late-19th-century architecture, and animals, of which there are a great many charming examples.

The view of American life provided by mechanical banks is as varied and interesting as the times they depict. They offer a mini-history of the United States to child and adult alike.

The market

Factors of rarity, condition, action, and authenticity influence the active and growing market for mechanical banks. Rarity is the first criterion, for although thousands of most banks were undoubtedly made, there are a number of which only two or three examples are known to exist today. Curiously, the bank most desired by collectors, the "Freedman" (1880), made by Jerome Secor, of Bridgeport, Connecticut, is not the rarest, indicating that other factors, notably action, play an important role in determining desirability.

Condition, always an element, is less important in the rare banks, increasingly significant in the more common examples. Both the casting itself, which is surprisingly fragile, and the paint, are essential aspects of a bank's condition. A bank with little paint, or worse, a repainted bank or a recast figure, lessen the value considerably.

Fakes are a significant problem for bank collectors. Most easily detected are the banks initially made as reproductions but later aged to appear original. A large group of these come from the "Book of Knowledge" castings, which were clearly marked with an indentation in the baseplate. These have been filed down by unscrupulous dealers and frequently are passed off as originals.

Less easily detected are those banks recast from original parts. Since they are made from parts, and not the patterns themselves, these banks are somewhat smaller than originals, and comparison between the base of such a recast bank and a genuine specimen is often the only certain way to determine that it is not authentic.

Neither of these categories of reproductions has any monetary value in the mechanical-bank market, and new collectors are wise to educate themselves before making any purchases by reading the available literature, and more importantly, by looking at originals. ∎

John Hall was a prolific designer for the Stevens Co. Above: *Hall's Excelsior Bank*—a tug at the doorbell and up pops the cashier. Manufactured in 1869, it is the oldest mechanical bank design. Below: *Tammany Bank*, designed by Hall in 1873 to satirize New York's infamous Boss Tweed. The bronze model for making molds is shown, left; the finished bank, right. All courtesy the Seamen's Bank for Savings; photos Mysak/Studio Nine.

Disc Music Boxes

Once the playthings of the very rich, resonant music boxes were available to all by the end of the 19th century, thanks to technological advances and mass production.

BY MADELINE ROGERS AND JOEL LEVINE

Today it is commonplace to pick up a music box in the five-and-dime. You find them among cheap toys and arcade novelties. But from the late 18th century, when the music box as we know it was invented, until the late 19th century, music boxes were playthings reserved for the rich and aristocratic of Europe. These so-called cylinder boxes, made chiefly in Switzerland, were named for the pin-studded cylinder that picked a comb to produce sound. Making these cylinder boxes involved the hand labor of skilled craftsmen.

To make the cylinder alone involved deciding where the pins were to be positioned; drilling tiny holes and inserting the pins one by one; filing them off and finally adjusting each pin by bending it individually so that the chords fell perfectly. Since even the tiniest cylinder mechanism—the sort often found in watches and snuffboxes of the time—had hundreds of pins, it is easy to understand why these mechanisms were too costly for any but the very rich.

By the end of the 19th century, music-box owners were no longer a select group; technical advancements made it possible to mass-produce complex, resonant music boxes using industrial methods.

The two most important developments were the disc and the star wheel. The first invention was a thin metal disc punched with tiny projections which served the same purpose as the hand-set pins on cylinder boxes—that is, they plucked the teeth of a comb to produce musical tones.

The roots of this invention are attributed to Miguel Boom, an enigmatic figure whose only claim to fame is his name on an 1882 disc-system patent.

Boom's invention was never put into production, but his concept was incorporated in one form or another in all later disc systems.

The problem with Boom's invention was that the combs were plucked directly by the disc projections. To do this consistently and accurately, the disc had to be finely tooled and quite thick, so that it would not bend.

To overcome these drawbacks with their consequent expense, Paul Wendland, an engineer at Germany's Symphonion Musikwerke, developed the star wheel. In a disc box there is one of these small, toothed wheels for each tooth of the comb. As the disc turns, its stamped projections, each representing a note, pass over the star wheels, which, in turn, pluck the notes to be played.

The importance of the star wheel was that it allowed the music-box manufacturer to use a thin, inexpensive machine-made disc without worrying about irregularities. Imperfections that would be critical if the projections had to connect directly with the comb were much less significant when the star wheel functioned as an intermediary.

The star wheel permitted the inexpensive mass production of discs and opened the doors to a new industry that led a charmed—albeit brief—life. The appeal of factory-made music boxes went beyond mere availability. Because they were mass produced, the disc boxes were considerably less expensive than their cylinder forebears.

Describing the way consumers viewed the old cylinder boxes, an article in a supplement to *Music Trade Review*, a trade journal of the period, dated April 30, 1898, noted: "The people wearied of the sameness in the matter of tunes and the constant necessity of repairs. It was hardly looked upon as a musical instrument, in fact, it was considered more as a toy."

Disc boxes were much more versatile. Unlike cylinders, which were fixed and usually programmed to play just a few tunes, discs could be changed the way we change records today. The number of selections was limited only by the number of discs available.

Disc boxes were first made in Europe by Symphonion, the company that originated the star wheel. That firm soon had competition from Polyphon, a company founded in 1890 by a former Symphonion foreman, skilled Gustave Brachhausen, and one of the firm's engineers, Paul Reissner.

The disc music box took many forms. Opposite right: The Regina Automatic Changer, ca 1898, complete with stained glass and a Seth Thomas clock. Courtesy Rita Ford Antique Music Boxes, New York. Opposite left: Symphonion, ca 1888, made by the Symphonion Company, the first firm to produce disc boxes. Courtesy Vicki Glasgow Antique Music Boxes, Scarsdale, New York.

Above left: *Thornwood*, made by Mermod Freres, a Swiss firm, ca 1900. Photo courtesy Vicki Glasgow Antique Music Boxes: Above right: In this old photograph members of the Regina Finishing Department proudly pose. Several men smartly display the different size bed plates they made for installation in an amazing variety of cases such as the elaborate parlor model automatic changer shown on the first page of this article, and the more modest table models. The Regina Music Box Company, located in Rahway, New Jersey, was the first music box company in the United States. Between 1894 and 1921 Regina sold about 100,000 instruments.

Though Europe—and particularly Switzerland and Germany—always had been the center of music-box manufacture, it was inevitable that the newer, more "democratic" disc boxes should come to America and its vast, middle-class market. In 1892 Brachhausen set up a Polyphon branch in the United States, dubbed the Regina Music Box Company.

Brachhausen's move may have been prompted by the uncertain tariff situation that prevailed at the time. In about 1887 Congress began to consider new tariff laws that would protect local industry by discouraging foreign imports. Although there is no direct evidence linking Brachhausen's emigration with the tariff situation, articles appearing at the time in *Music Trade Review* indicate that the music business as a whole was concerned about the future of imports into this country. Seeing a potentially large market threatened by impending tariff legislation, Brachhausen may well have decided to exploit the market before it was closed to him.

We do know that by 1897, when the Dingley law levied a 45 percent duty on imported musical instruments, Regina was already three years old and well established in Rahway, New Jersey.

Like all successful endeavors, Regina soon gave rise to a number of competitors. One of the first was F. G. Otto & Sons, a company that had been in the business of making surgical instruments and electrical batteries. Though it used a star wheel and comb arrangement similar to Regina's, the Otto firm may have been trying to avert a patent infringement suit by coming up with its "capital cuff," a cone-shaped, perforated record that took the place of the flat disc.

If that was their intention, it did not work. Regina sued Otto, setting off a flurry of legal battles. Soon the industry was so rife with suits and countersuits that in one ruling against Regina a judge opined: "It is to be hoped that the music-box interests which have become such a flourishing American industry in a comparatively short time, may soon be relieved from the very detrimental atmosphere of patent suits to which they have been subjected almost from the start."

Regina's other major competitor was Symphonion. Like Regina, its roots were in Germany, where, in 1885 or 1886, its parent company introduced the first disc box with interchangeable discs. About ten years later Symphonion of Germany provided backing for an American subsidiary, the Symphonion Manufacturing Company.

During its brief history, the American music-box industry—the three companies described above, plus numerous smaller firms that were as evanescent as a music-box tune—made hundreds of music-box styles, shapes and sizes. Q. David Bowers in *Encyclopedia of Automatic Musical Instruments* estimates that between 1894 and 1921 Regina alone had sold about 100,000 instruments. (Those interested in a survey of specific styles of boxes will find a comprehensive one in this book, obtainable from The Vestal Press, Box 97, 320 N. Jensen Rd., Vestal, N.Y. 13850.)

Boxes usually were categorized according to the size of the

Far left: The Criterion, ca 1898, made by F.G. Otto & Sons. Middle: Another type of case is this grandfather clock made by Seth Thomas; the Regina bed plate is visible through its glass door. The clock can be set to play music on the hour, or whenever desired. Below: Another unusually styled case is this smoking cabinet case. Called the Britania, it was made by B.H. Abrahams, a Swiss firm, about 1898. All photos courtesy Vicki Glasgow Antique Music Boxes.

disc and the number of combs, which together determine the number of notes a box can play and the richness and volume of sound. Regina boxes, for instance, were made in three main sizes: 15½-inch, 20¾-inch and 27-inch. The two larger sizes usually were fitted with two combs, called the duplex comb style. The smaller size offered a choice of two combs or a cheaper one-comb version.

Throughout the industry the basic mechanism was fitted into a bewildering variety of case sizes and styles that reflected the taste of the times. The most popular American music box was doubtless the Regina Model 11, made continuously from 1894 through the early 20th century. This table model, "equipped with duplex music combs and housed in a compact case, was the logical instrument for the average customer to purchase," according to Bowers. It was priced at about $75. In addition to simple table models like the Regina Model 11, American music-box manufacturers turned out novelty boxes of all kinds.

Music box mechanisms also were sold to other sorts of manufacturing concerns for inclusion in their products. The musical grandfather clocks made by Seth Thomas, for example, contained the Regina mechanism.

In addition to home models, American music-box manufacturers also built large upright boxes outfitted with coin slots for use in public places. These magnificent instruments, in their ornate cases, often fitted with glass panels for advertising inscriptions, were the equivalent of the modern jukebox. They commonly were found in retail stores, ice cream parlors, taverns, and hotel lobbies. By about 1905, the player piano, with its greater volume, had largely replaced the music box in these locations.

Two disadvantages of the disc music box in commercial locations—the need to wind it frequently and the need to change discs frequently were overcome when Regina introduced its Automatic Changer in 1898. This instrument could automatically play 12 discs, for up to 40 minutes. On April 30, 1898, *Music Trade Review* remarked that "its value as an entertainer in public buildings, halls, schools, coast steamers, railway depots, stores, or in the home is . . . apparent . . . and we cannot but predict a big demand for it in due course."

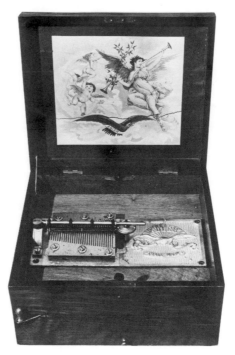

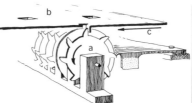

Above left: Regina automatic, ca 1898. This large instrument holds 27 half-inch discs and stores twelve of them in a storage rack inside the cabinet. The twelve discs play automatically, in sequence, or may be individually selected with a dial. Photo courtesy Rita Ford Antique Music Boxes. Middle: In this table model Adler, made by J.H. Zimmerman, ca 1900, one can easily see the bed-plate on which the disc is placed. The bar across the top of the plate holds the disc in place. Right: *The Euphonia*, made by F.G. Otto & Sons, is unusual for its art nouveau case. Courtesy Vicki Glasgow.

Left: Drawing of the star wheel. Along with the development of the disc, the star wheel revolutionized the music box industry in the late 1880s. Not only were the star-wheel models less expensive to produce than the old cylinder boxes, but they could play more than one tune. In a disc box, the tuned steel teeth of the comb are struck by the points of the star wheel to make music. The star wheel is activated by the projections on the underside of the disc. The disc is held against the star wheel by a bar with pressure rollers. Here, the star wheel (a) is shown with one point against a projection of the disc (b) and another point against a tooth of the comb (c), shown in cross-section. Drawing by Richard Zoehrer.

The fact that America could nurture an industry that had been rooted for so long in Europe was noted with patriotic pride in the July 21, 1897, issue of *Music Trade Review*, which remarked that customers were "amazed almost to the point of admiration at the enterprise of those who have undertaken to reproduce, with additional mechanical and musical effects, goods, hitherto exclusively foreign in every particular."

The fires of chauvinism were fed by the brief Spanish-American War fought during the spring and summer of 1898. The war turned America's attention to its homegrown industries. In the case of the music-box industry, it spurred the introduction of a new music-box model and spawned an innovative advertising campaign for the product—the Olympia music box made by F. G. Otto.

On May 1, 1898, Commodore George Dewey won the battle of Manila Bay from his ship, the *Olympia*. On May 28, Otto announced to the trade a new line of music boxes known as the Olympia, taking its name directly from Dewey's flagship. The first advertisement for the box ran in *Music Trade Review*. It read, "Dewey won at Manila with the flagship

Olympia. The enterprising music dealer can win against trade competition with the Olympia." Two months later, the product was unveiled to the public and by October 15, 1898, Otto was placing similar ads in popular consumer magazines.

At about the same time, in August, 1898, *Music Trade Review* gleefully reported that Spanish officers had an Otto "Criterion" music box in their headquarters and had one tune they particularly liked. It wasn't until the surrender ceremonies at the close of the war that the red-faced officers realized that the tune they had played repeatedly was the enemy's national anthem—"The Star-Spangled Banner."

At this point the American music-box industry was at its peak and looking ahead to a rosy future. In the September 18, 1897, issue of *Music Trade Review*, for example, an editorial suggested that "[the] adoption of [Regina boxes] in doctors' and dentists' offices will make the patient's visit a pleasure. This is a happy thought. People have been yearning all along for just such results and the day is not far distant, let us hope, when every surgeon and every dentist desiring to establish and maintain a lucrative practice shall provide soothing melodies for the comfort of his constituents."

While the sentiment was lovely, it was never fulfilled. The late 19th century was a time of feverish invention and industrial expansion. Just as the disc music box closed down the Swiss cylinder-box industry, it was inevitable that something would come along and usurp the disc box.

That something was the Gramophone.

By the early 1900s it was obvious that this new invention, as embryonic and imperfect as it was, was a serious threat to music boxes. Some companies tried to adjust by producing combination instruments that could function both as a music box and a phonograph. Eventually the three largest music-box companies in the world—Symphonion, Polyphon, and Regina—went into the phonograph business.

Q. David Bowers in his *Encyclopedia of Automatic Musical Instruments* provides a poignant footnote to the short but great history of the American music-box industry:

If Gustave Brachhausen had been in a different frame of mind one day soon after the turn of the century, Regina's history might have been vastly different. A certain Eldridge R. Johnson called on Brachhausen and the principals of Regina and tried to interest them in the new lateral-cut phonograph disc. . . . It was a revolutionary approach, as the Edison machines used cylinders on which the grooves were cut vertically. Brachhausen listened briefly, scoffed at the idea, and sent the fellow on his way. . . . Johnson went home to Camden, New Jersey, and founded the Victor Talking Machine Company. Sales in 1901, the first year, amounted to just $500. Four years later sales were $12,000,000. In 1921, the year that Regina shipped its last instruments, Victor sales were $51,000,000! ■

You have found the disc music box of your dreams and are tempted to buy it. Before you do, find out as much as possible about its condition. Repairs can be costly, and in some cases are not feasible.

First, establish whether the music box runs. If it has a good sound, chances are that the vital parts are intact and need only a good cleaning.

If the box runs but sounds out of tune, you may be committing yourself to an expensive repair job. Tuning a music box is not as easy as tuning a piano. Music boxes were designed to stay in tune permanently. When they fail, it usually means that there is serious rust or corrosion on the comb. This is a condition that is difficult, though not impossible, to correct. It is a tedious job that can be done only by an expert.

A music box that runs but produces rasping, buzzing, or clicking sounds may have missing or damaged dampers. Dampers are slivers of brass or steel, activated by the star wheel, that stop the sound of a vibrating note so that it can be repeated quickly and cleanly. If a note's vibration is not stopped by the damper, a buzz results, making mechanical music sound even more mechanical.

While it is possible to replace missing dampers, the cost escalates with the number of dampers missing. For some of the rarer models of music boxes it may be impossible to find replacements. When in doubt, check with an expert.

If the music box is not running, the job of deciding just what it is you are buying becomes more difficult. There are three common reasons for breakdowns: a broken spring, damaged or missing parts, or dirt in the mechanism. If you can, look inside the mechanism. Check to see that the whole drive train is intact and that none of the gears is damaged. If gears are damaged, replacement is expensive, as they must be custom made.

In a machine that is not running, you will still have to check for dampers and tuning. To do this, rotate a disc by hand and listen to a few chords, checking for foreign noises and tuning. Make sure that the disc you are playing is one made for that machine. Some discs work on more than one type of machine; others don't. Some that are interchangeable are: Regina-Polyphon, Olympia-Criterion, Symphonion—Imperial Symphonion.

If you are buying one of the rarer machines—for instance, Triumph, Monarch, Perfection—be sure you get a good supply of discs with it. They are hard to come by. Discs for Regina and Polyphon, on the other hand, are currently being reissued.

While poking around in the mechanism, check the star wheels. These are the devices that transmit the disc's "message" to the comb(s). There should be one star wheel for every tooth in a comb. They should rotate freely within their frames and none of their points should be damaged. If the star wheels and/or their frames are rusted or corroded to the point of being frozen, repair may be prohibitively expensive.

Look too for broken teeth on the comb. It is possible to replace teeth, but once again, the costs are high. One or two teeth may be replaced for a modest fee, but when whole sections of teeth are broken, the costs escalate quickly.

If you find a music box that is missing ten teeth but is in good running order and has a mint-condition case and 25 discs, repairing it may be worthwhile.

However, if the piece doesn't work, has a case that looks like it has been soaking in brine, and comes with six badly rusted discs and 25 broken teeth, you may be better off paying more for a music box in better condition.

As to the condition of discs, watch for broken projections on the underside. Each broken projection is a lost note. Look, too, for enlarged center holes and broken outer sprocket holes.

Before making an expensive purchase, look at as many boxes as you can. These are not complicated machines. Armed with some knowledge, freed from dependence on luck, you are more likely to find a machine that will provide hours of listening pleasure.

Oil Burning Lamps

Though candlelight is romantic and candle-holders have been made in many styles, oil-burning lamps brought significant improvements to artificial lighting in the United States. The extraordinary fact about the oil lamp is that its form changed only slightly in thousands of years.

BY JOSEPH T. BUTLER

From the days of open fires and torches, men have been preoccupied with the problem of illuminating their houses. Eventually they discovered that a simple saucer-shaped vessel filled with animal fat could fuel a crude wick made from a piece of reed or bundle of hair. This convenient method of lighting could be carried everywhere.

The pottery and bronze lamps of the Egyptians, Greeks, and Romans hardly bettered this fundamental principle. Refined wicks made from hemp or cotton and the use of vegetable oil rather than animal fat were the only improvements. In Europe the wick lamp persisted through the Middle Ages. Even Renaissance civilization, with its many scientific discoveries, did not contribute much to lamp technology.

By the late 16th or early 17th centuries, a metal trough or channel was used inside the lamp to hold the wick in place and directly connected it with the shallow reservoir. *Float lamps*—in which the wick was attached to a cork floating directly on a reservoir of oil—were also used then. Vigil lamps in churches were often of this type.

17-century American lamps

In 17th-century America, early settlers used the same simple type of oil lamp. A deposit of bog iron, discovered about 1630 in the town of Saugus, Massachusetts, provided the source for iron production. Lamps probably were made there. The simplest type of American 17th-century lamp, called a *crusie* or *phoebe*, was an iron pan-shaped vessel for fat or oil in which a wick was laid. Sometimes a second pan was used, to double the amount of light. A metal hook with sharpened end was often attached to such a lamp so it could be hung or thrust into a beam. Another type of early light, the *betty*, may have derived its name from the German *besser*, meaning "better." This type of lamp had a hinged lid, reducing the possibility of the wick igniting the oil, as well as the previously mentioned iron channel to hold the wick in place. Betty lamps burned grease or oil from small fish abundant in the coastal waters.

The betty and crusie lamps did not disappear with the end of the 17th century. Indeed, lamps of this simplest type, made of iron, tinned sheet metal, and pottery, have a long history of use extending in rural places into the 20th century. Henry Mercer of Doylestown, Pennsylvania, wrote in *Light and Fire Making* (1898) that he had observed betty lamps in daily use in farming homes in his area. He even gives directions for filling such a lamp: "Thrust the point horizontally into a beam or catch the barb upon a hook, nail, or log crevice, then, filling the vessel with lard, light the twisted cotton wick, laid along the internal trough, so tilted as to allow the oil oozing from the flame to flow back into the vessel." These lamps gave only a dim flicker of light. Because of their offensive smoke and unpleasant odors, betty lamps were probably used only when necessary.

The Argand lamp

During most of the 18th century in America, candles—used in

The availability of kerosene spurred the development of artificial light. By the late 1860's kerosene lamps were manufactured in glass (like the example here) and in pottery, brass and bronze. Private collection.

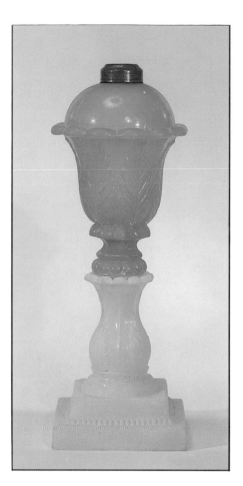

sticks, chandeliers, sconces, and floor stands—dominated lighting. But in 1783 a Swiss chemist named Amié Argand developed the first lamp constructed on principles of scientific combustion. This lamp embodied a hollow wick holder open at both ends, which extended upward through the center of the burner. A closely woven cylindrical wick was fitted tightly around the tube, and an outer cylinder was placed around this. Oil from the reservoir reached the wick in two ways. In one type, the reservoir was placed higher than the burner so that gravity forced it to the wick; in the other, the reservoir was placed below the wick and the oil rose in it. The hollow tube in the center served to admit air to the center of the flame, increasing combustion and the amount of light. Heat from the flame created a draft, which was enhanced by the addition of a glass chimney. These lamps burned refined whale oil, which was increasingly available.

In both shape and decoration, Argand lamps reflect the neoclassical style of the very late 18th century. Both George Washington and Thomas Jefferson were known to use lamps of this type. One of Sheffield plate, owned by George Washington, is presently at Mount Vernon. It is shaped like an urn, incorporating the Argand burner with chimney directly in its center over the reservoir. The Argand burner was used in fixtures with varying numbers of arms made for tables and mantelpieces, as hanging lamps, and as wall brackets. Some exam-

ples were fitted with parts made from Wedgwood pottery, which heightened the neoclassical effect of the form. An interesting document is the portrait *James Peale, the Miniature Painter* by his brother, Charles Willson Peale, painted in 1822. The subject is studying a miniature by the light of an Argand lamp, incorporating both a glass chimney and a shade, that has a Wedgwood drum set into the base. This type of lamp continued to be used until the mid-19th century.

Both Baldwin Gardiner and Christian Cornelius, the two best-remembered American manufacturers of Argand lamps, began their careers as silversmiths. Gardiner founded the bronze-casting firm of Fletcher and Gardiner in Philadelphia and eventually moved to New York, where he managed his own firm between 1827 and 1845. Argand lamps labeled "B. Gardiner, New York," generally of high quality, show the movement from the classical to rococo revival styles. The firm founded by Cornelius went through a succession of names—C. Cornelius & Son; Cornelius & Co. and finally Cornelius and Baker. Their lamps were also of excellent quality; by 1845 Cornelius was the largest producer of lamps in America. The firm retained its importance until the end of the century.

After an initial invention is made, other improvements rapidly follow. In 1787, John Miles of Birmingham, England, patented his "agitable" burner, a simple device of no great

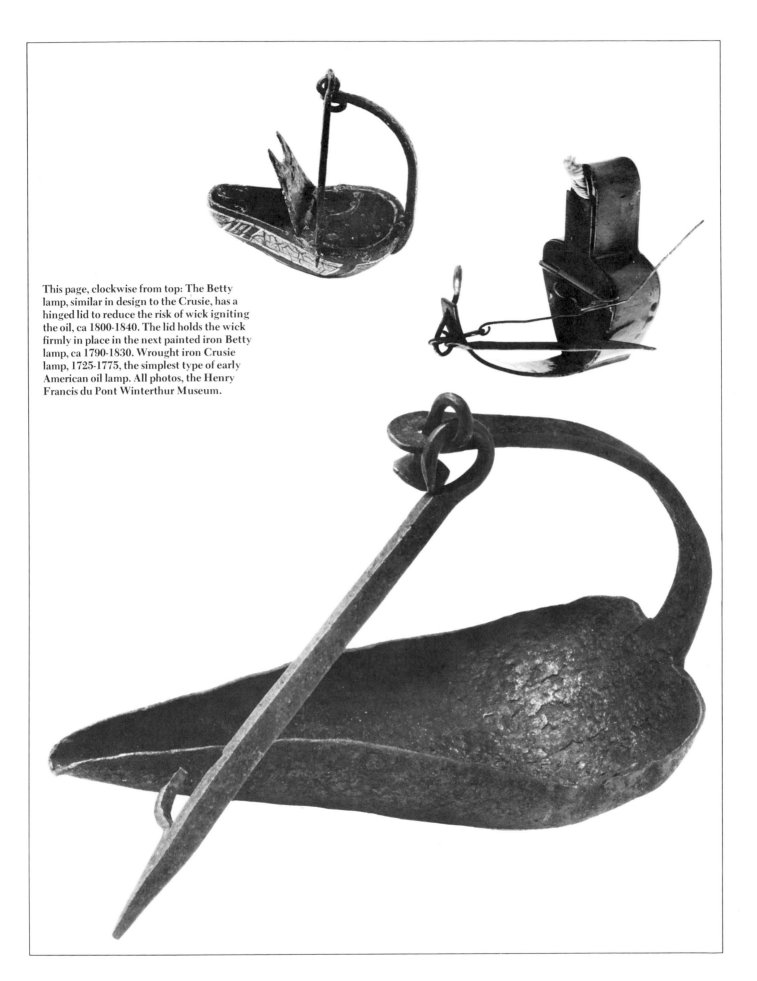

This page, clockwise from top: The Betty lamp, similar in design to the Crusie, has a hinged lid to reduce the risk of wick igniting the oil, ca 1800-1840. The lid holds the wick firmly in place in the next painted iron Betty lamp, ca 1790-1830. Wrought iron Crusie lamp, 1725-1775, the simplest type of early American oil lamp. All photos, the Henry Francis du Pont Winterthur Museum.

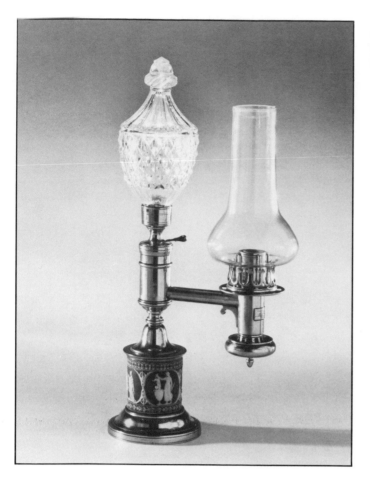

scientific principle. The lamp was simply a container with a hole at the top into which a burner with one or more metal wick tubes was screwed or tightly fitted. The container was filled with whale oil, which was drawn upward through the vertical wicks.

The whaling industry, well-established when Miles developed his burner, expanded further after 1800 due to the increasing popularity of whale-oil lamps. By 1830 the average American home boasted at least one whale-oil lamp. Glass factories in New England and the Midwest mass-produced whale-oil lamps in great quantities, while others were made in brass, pewter, and tinned sheet metal. An interesting variant is the peg lamp, made of metal with a bottom peg which could be placed in a candlestick, thus converting the stick to a lamp.

Camphene burners

In 1830 Isaiah Jennings patented a new fuel that he called *burning fluid* a combination of alcohol and spirits of turpentine in a proportion of eight to one. The burner for this fluid resembled the whale-oil burner, but the two metal wick tubes slanted away from each other because of the highly inflammable fuel.

In 1830, the year the new fuel was patented, the *Franklin Institute Journal* commented:

> We have seen the above mixture in combustion in an Argand's lamp. The flame was clear, dense, and brilliant. The light may

be made greatly to exceed that from oil, without the escape of any smoke, and there is not the slightest odor of turpentine. The patentee says the mixture is as cheap as spermaceti oil, and that he is making arrangements which will enable him to afford it at less cost considerably below that material. The friends of temperance will not object to the burning of alcohol.

However, by 1834, the *Franklin Institute Journal* had reversed its opinion. Camphene, as it was later called, was discovered to be dangerous to use:

> The late fatal accidents resulting from the use of such ingredients in lamps will, however, probably put a final stop to the use of these mixtures, and we have no doubt that a court of law would now decide that they are not useful, within the meaning of the statute.

Newspapers from the first half of the 19th century recorded many camphene-related accidents. Typical is this account from *Scientific American* of June 19, 1847: "Miss Mary Watson was burned to death in Philadelphia last week, while attempting to fill a fluid lamp when it was burning, and the liquid taking fire caused the catastrophe. Her mother and brother, who were in the room, were badly burned in attempting to save her."

Other lamp variations

The Rumford lamps are rare in America. Count Rumford was born in 1753 as Benjamin Thompson of Woburn, Massachusetts. A tory who fought against the Colonies, he was knighted by George III at the end of the Revolutionary War. He later

The Argand lamps opposite reflect the neo-classic style of the early 19th century. Opposite, left: Brass and glass Argand lamp with a Wedgewood Jasparware mount, 1825-1875. The Henry Francis duPont Winterthur Museum. The hollow wick holder, open at both ends, extends upward through the burner, allowing air to flow through the center of the wick. This insures a steady, bright light from the flame. Opposite, right: Sheffield plate Argand lamp owned by George Washington. The chimney of the Argand burner is in the center, over the urn-shaped reservoir. Mount Vernon Ladies' Association.

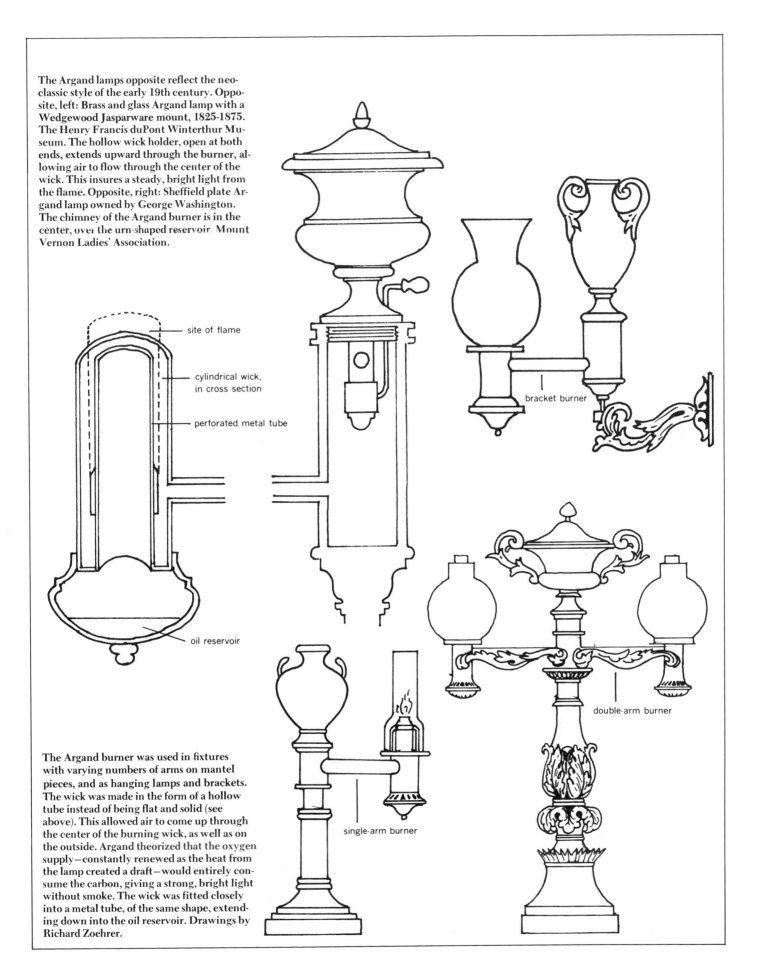

site of flame

cylindrical wick, in cross section

perforated metal tube

oil reservoir

bracket burner

double-arm burner

single-arm burner

The Argand burner was used in fixtures with varying numbers of arms on mantel pieces, and as hanging lamps and brackets. The wick was made in the form of a hollow tube instead of being flat and solid (see above). This allowed air to come up through the center of the burning wick, as well as on the outside. Argand theorized that the oxygen supply—constantly renewed as the heat from the lamp created a draft—would entirely consume the carbon, giving a strong, bright light without smoke. The wick was fitted closely into a metal tube, of the same shape, extending down into the oil reservoir. Drawings by Richard Zoehrer.

joined the court of Prince Maximilian of Bavaria, where he became a count of the Holy Roman Empire. His title—Rumford—was derived from the old name for Concord, New Hampshire, where he once lived. When Rumford invented his lamp is not certain: it was probably during the last years of the 18th century. A Rumford lamp, generally made of tole (painted tin), had a wide wick with a rack-and-pinion raider, an oil reservoir on the level of the top of the wick tube, a chimney, and a shade.

The French improved the Argand principle with the annular lamp. In this type, the oil reservoir is moved so that it fits under the shade and is circular in shape. The fuel, refined whale oil, ran from the reservoir through two fuel tubes into the wick. The lamp incorporated an Argand-type burner.

During the 1830s and 1840s the lamp most popularly used on elegant parlor tables in the United States was the so-called astral. It utilized an Argand burner placed above an axially located oil reservoir with air holes around its base. Frosted and cut-glass shades were generally on the brass or bronze bases. An improved version, the *sinumbra* ("without shadow") lamp introduced a ring-shaped reservoir. This allowed the light to fall directly below without interference from the reservoir. The names *astral* and *sinumbra* sometimes are used interchangeably. These lamps, which continued to be popular until mid-century, burned whale oil. They were made of bronze, brass, and sometimes silver or pressed glass.

Another type, the *solar*, was related to the astral lamp. It was designed to burn lard in a modified Argand burner patented by Cornelius & Co. in 1843. The lard reservoir was placed directly under the flame, and a saucer-shaped draft de-

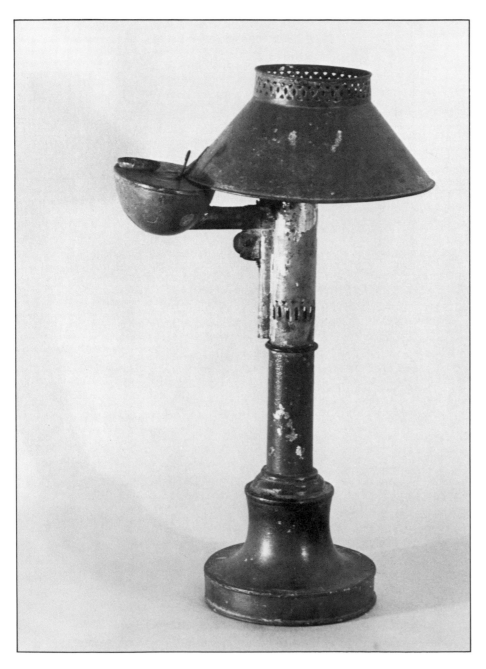

flector positioned above the wick shaded the flame so that it became a beam of light. The economical and efficient solar lamp was popular at the same time as the astral lamp.

In the years following 1830, scientists and inventors vied with one another to develop and patent more efficient types of lamps. This extraordinary activity is recorded in the Patent Office in Washington. Rosin, lard, and refinements of whale oil were fuels most commonly used in these experimental lamps.

The Carcel or mechanical lamp, named for its inventor, was patented in France in 1800 but did not become popular in the United States until about 1850. It used an Argand burner with an elaborate clockwork pump mechanism that controlled a spring-driven pump, forcing oil to the top of the burner. The whale oil burned in these lamps produced an in-

tense light, protected by a vertical chimney and globe-shaped shade. Most Carcel lamps used in the United States were imported from France and therefore were costly.

Kerosene lamps

The development of kerosene was probably the single most important innovation in artificial lighting. The fuel, named kerosene by Abraham Gesner of Williamsburg, New York, was known in America as early as 1824. In fact, this fuel was known in antiquity. But it was never popular until the development of Pennsylvania oil fields in the late 1850s and 1860s made it generally affordable. By 1866, 28 million gallons of kerosene, or "coal oil," were distilled a year.

No one knows who invented the kerosene burner or the steps leading to it. Its woven-cloth wick is flat and can be

Opposite page left: Rumford Lamp, ca 1850, japanned tinned sheet iron. Opposite right: Carcel lamp, bronze and glass, ca 1840. Both, Sleepy Hollow Restorations, Tarrytown, New York. This page, left: Astral lamp Cornelius & Company, 1843. Bronze and gilt with frosted cut glass shade. Newark Museum Collection. Right: Sinumbra lamp with candle arms, 1790-1820, silverplate with cut and frosted glass shade. The Henry Francis du Pont Winterthur Museum.

raised or lowered by a spur at the side. A dome-shaped cap or deflector of brass protects the wick and generally was fitted with prongs to hold a cylindrical glass chimney. Globular and half-globular glass shades were often used in combination with the chimney to filter the light. By the last quarter of the century, cloth and paper shades were in use on such lamps. Kerosene lamps were made from a great variety of materials—glass, pottery, brass, bronze, and many metallic alloys. Design of kerosene lamps often reflects the eclecticism and historicism that characterized late-19th-century design.

One type of kerosene lamp, the Hitchcock lamp, was developed to be used with a flat wick, but without a chimney or shade. These lamps had a spring-driven motor to provide the necessary draft to the flame. A lamp of this type was patented previously in England in 1840 and later in the United States. But Robert Hitchcock acquired the patents and produced these lamps in Watertown, New York. Other American factories also produced lamps of this type.

Mass production greatly affected the quality of the kerosene lamp, which was now available to everyone. The higher quality seen earlier in the century in beautiful castings and glass shades disappeared. By the early years of the 20th century, the age of oil had come to an end and was superseded by electricity. ■

Above, left: Hitchcock Lamp, fueled by kerosene, was designed to be used shadeless. This example was made ca 1875 by Joseph M. Bailey and George A. Jones, New York. Greenfield Village and Henry Ford Museum. Whale oil lamps were made in various forms. The pewter model, (opposite top, right), has double magnifying lenses. The New-York Historical Society; gift of John V. Irwin. Opposite top, left: Tin whale oil lamp, early 19th century. The New-York Historical Society. Above, right: The camphene lamp burned a volatile mixture of alcohol and turpentine. Wood, ca 1850. Old Sturbridge Village; photos Henry E. Peach. Opposite: *James Peale the Miniature Painter* by Charles Willson Peale, 1822. The artist's brother studies his work by the light of an Argand lamp, invented in 1793. The Detroit Institute of Art.

Index

About the Authors

HEIDI L. BERRY is a freelance writer and collector.

JOSEPH T. BUTLER is curator and director of collections at Sleepy Hollow Restorations, Tarrytown, New York.

MARGARET MATTISON COFFIN is a recognized tinware authority and has written many articles on the subject.

RUFUS FOSHEE, a Maine antiques dealer, specializes in moch-aware and other types of pottery.

JOHN P. GUTTENBERG, JR., writes on Americana.

HELEN HARRIS is antiques editor for *Town & Country* magazine.

JUDITH A. JEDLICKA, a folk art collector, is Executive Director of The Fund for the Dance and contributing editor to *Horizon* magazine.

KATHLEEN EAGEN JOHNSON is the registrar at Sleepy Hollow Restorations in Tarrytown, New York.

JOEL LEVINE repairs music boxes professionally.

CATHERINE LYNN, author of *Wallpaper in America*, teaches American decorative arts at the university level.

SUSAN E. MEYER, formerly editorial director of *Art & Antiques* magazine, is the author of several books on art and design.

A. J. PELUSO, JR. is the author of *J. & J. Bard, Picture Painters* (Hudson River Press, 1977).

DANIEL PRINCE is a Connecticut-based writer.

MADELINE ROGERS is a New York-based writer specializing in antiques and home furnishings.

RICHARD F. SNOW is the managing editor of *American Heritage* magazine and a frequent writer on Americana.

BONNIE BARRETT STRETCH is a writer and photographer living in New York.

RUTH AMDUR TANENHAUS, a former curator, is a freelance writer.